ISSUES IN CHURCH AND SOCIETY IN AFRICA

Tackling for Growth and Inclusion

ISSUES IN CHURCH AND SOCIETY IN AFRICA

Tackling for Growth and Inclusion

BY

Evaristus Bassey

Caritas Nigeria Publications

NIHIL OBSTAT: Fr. Ojaje Idoko

Copyright © 2016 Evaristus Bassey

Published by Caritas Nigeria Press, Abuja

ISBN-978-978-954-854-5

NATIONAL LIBRARY OF NIGERIA CATALOGUING-IN-PUBLICATION DATA
BASSEY, Evaristus
Issues in Church and Society in Africa: Tackling for Growth and Inclusion.
1. Church and the world – Catholic Church. I. Title
BV 625 B 319 2015 201.72

CONDITIONS OF SALES

DEDICATION

This book is dedicated to Cardinal Anthony Okogie, Cardinal John Oniayekan, Archbishop Ignatius Kaigama, Emeritus Archbishop Job, Emeritus Archbishop Joseph E. Ukpo, Archbishop Joseph E. Ekuwem, Archbishop A. Obinna, Bishop Lucius Ugorji and Bishop Matthew Kukah, for all efforts they and other Bishops are putting into making Nigeria and Africa better.

ACKNOWLEDGEMENT

I sincerely thank Archbishop Joseph E. Ukpo, for providing me an opportunity to serve at the Catholic Bishops Conference of Nigeria and my incumbent archbishop, Most Rev. Joseph E. Ekuwem for always giving me a listening ear. I thank all my colleagues at the Catholic Secretariat of Nigeria, and the cooperation and commitment of Caritas Nigeria staff. I acknowledge the efforts of my friends and relatives: Joe Edet and Emma Ntuyang. I thank Almighty God for all the undeserved blessings.

CONTENTS CONTENTS

AUTHOR'S PREFACE

This book is actually a collection of essays, some of which were presentations I made in certain fora, while others were first published in magazines or newspapers. Many of the write-ups have been revised to factor in contemporary updates. Few of the essays may have cross cutting themes but their uniqueness is not removed.

As the title suggests, these essays are basically write-ups about social issues seen from the perspective of faith, the Catholic faith. The Catholic Church promotes a set of social principles which align with all religions. No religion hates the poor for instance, and none is anti-common good of society, except where a few adherents decide to misinterpret aspects of their scripture. In other words the issues treated here reverberate with everyone whether Christian or not.

As my 50th anniversary on earth was coming close, I thought that it was best to have a memorial. Putting together in one volume some of these essays or presentations which I had made in the last few years seemed to be the most attractive and viable option.

I am therefore delighted to offer this buffet menu of sorts.

Please be enriched.

Fr. Evaristus A. Bassey
Abuja 2016

CHAPTER ONE

FEEDING A STRANGER A DAY: HUNGER AND CO-RESPONSIBILITY IN A CHANGING SOCIETY

At the September 2013 United Nations General Assembly, the world was making a great transition from working towards reducing poverty to a commitment towards total eradication of poverty.   The Heads of States and Governments made the following declaration inter alia:

'We are resolved that the post-2015 development agenda should reinforce the international community's commitment to poverty eradication and sustainable development. We underscore the central imperative of poverty eradication and are committed to freeing humanity from poverty and hunger as a matter of urgency. Recognising the intrinsic interlinkage between poverty eradication and promotion of sustainable development, we underline the need for a coherent approach which integrates in a balanced manner the three dimensions of sustainable development. This coherent approach involves working towards a single framework and set of Goals -universal in nature and applicable to all countries, while taking account of differing national circumstances and respecting national policies and priorities. It should also promote peace and security, democratic governance, the rule of law, gender equality and human rights for all.'[1]

This declaration was concretised with the adoption of the Sustainable Development Goals two years later. Poverty eradication is put forward by this declaration, as the main thrust of governance, and every government is exhorted to take urgent steps towards its eradication with the massive social benefit of liberating humanity from poverty and its most terrible effect, hunger.

Here in this article, the thrust is the role of the individual as a change agent, especially in a context where institutions perform at their lowest capacities. Other writers have taken different approaches, for instance, on the role of the state in the provision of social safety nets.

The Nigerian Context

The July 2016 estimate of the population of Nigeria, according to Worldometers, puts it at 187,135,798. Of this, 48% are estimated to be urban dwellers with the balance dwelling in rural and semi rural environments[2]. A 2009 report of the International Food Policy Research Institute observed that "dwellers in rural areas are especially vulnerable to chronic food shortages, malnutrition, unbalanced nutrition, erratic food supply, poor quality foods, high food costs, and even total lack of food.[3a] This is even more worrisome when we consider that there appears to be a decline in the urbanization in some cities with more people now returning to the rural areas. Various factors such as high accommodation costs, frustrating job searches occasioned by the low employment rates and insecurity have led to many persons migrating back to their ancestral communities. For instance in the wake of the Boko Haram crises many Igbo traders have had to return home. The opposite effect has also been observed in some instances, where urban areas have witnessed population growth because of their relative security. Jos for instance has had a recent population growth as a result of influx of persons from areas with high levels of Boko Haram insurgency who see Jos city as being more secure.

Whether in the urban areas or rural areas, food access appears to be a challenge. A visit to some Catholic parishes in Abuja, Lagos or Port Harcourt where there is monthly or weekly food sharing to the needy will confirm the fact that many families have not conquered the basic need for food, which is a symptom of severe poverty. Where food is available it is quite expensive and unaffordable to many. In the October 2015 Food and Agricultural Organisation (FAO) Food security data for Nigeria, the average food deficit of undernourished populations out of the minimum dietary energy requirement of 1,730 kcal/person/day was 42kcal/person /day.[3b] Those of us who visit rural areas know that in certain communities, it is a great luxury to eat any mix of food three times a day, not to mention a balanced diet. Not only may the resources not be available, often there is ignorance as to what constitutes a balanced diet. Nutritional education therefore seems to be lacking even when there is food availability.

The Effects of Hunger

The effect of hunger is psychosomatic; not only does it affect the body, manifesting in stomach aches, headaches and weakness, 'it also takes a toll on our mood, our focus and our sense of physical well being'[4] Ultimately it has a severe impact on the economy.

Hunger affects learning in every age, especially children. 'Childhood malnutrition can cause reduced intelligence, anxiety, psychiatric issues and cognitive impairment in the long term.'[5] Deficiencies in certain vitamins like A could cause poor eye sight, while the lack of calcium could lead to poor gum and teeth formation. The optimal performance of the heart is weakened as hunger causes reduced oxygen levels and slow heart rate, leading to weakness. Such foods as calcium, iron, protein and Vitamin B are best for the performance of the heart, as indicated by Eluaka.[6] The internal organs also become affected when they don't have enough fibre from fruits, vegetables and whole grains. Insufficient Vitamin A could affect the skin and it begins to dry out and form flakes. Rather than be a protective cover for the body, it becomes like a dress with unpatched tears. The absence of protein severely affects the muscles, causing pains in joints and difficulty in physical exercise. Bone formation depends on calcium. A malnourished child will have weak bones for life. Above all hunger and malnutrition affect the immune system. Some diseases that are the immediate effect of malnutrition include scurvy (mostly in refugee populations, manifesting bruises and bleeding, hair and teeth loss, joint swellings and pain); wet and dry beri beri (shortness of breath, swellings, enlarged heart, shortness of breath, loss of feelings in hands, disproportionate eye movements, coma, vomiting etc), pellagra(diarrhea, disfiguring skin marks, dementia); Protein-Energy Malnutrition (PEM, commonly called Kwashiorkor or Marasmus - swollen abdomen, stunted growth, low weight, thin limbs and diarrhea etc).

In an advocacy tool of WHO entitled Turning The Tide of Nutrition: Responding to the Challenge of the 21st Century, the effects of poor nutrition are captured as follows:

- *Malnutrition kills, maims, cripples and blinds on a massive scale world wide*
- *Malnutrition affects one in every three people worldwide, afflicting all age groups and populations, especially the poor and vulnerable*
- *Malnutrition plays a major role in half of the 10.4 million annual child deaths in the developing world; it continues to be cause and consequence of disease disability in the children who survive.*
- *Malnutrition is not only medical it is also a social disorder rooted in poverty and discrimination.*

- *Malnutrition has economic ripple effects that can jeopardize development.[7]*

Seeing the effect of hunger we cannot but agree that if life is a fundamental human right, and food is absolutely necessary in sustaining it, then food is a right.

The Good Samaritan Paradigm

In Nigeria, a tendency is developing that could gradually affect co-responsibility as far as caring for the other is concerned; it is superstition. Superstition simply is the belief that certain events or situations occur without natural or logical explanation, 'belief that particular events bring good or bad luck.'[8] Not that superstition is new to Nigeria; as a traditional culture it is a prevalent feature. Perhaps through the popularization of single incidents by Africa Magic movie channels, and fear inculcated by the preaching of various brands of Pentecostal churches, rendering relief to the other, especially one who is relatively unknown, whether through cash or food or clothing, is gradually being seen by many as an investment in desolation. Many believe that persons with occult powers and influence pose as helpless and use the assistance they are given as a link to the wealth of the giver, feeding on and devouring the resources in a supernatural way until the giver becomes impoverished. This could account for why you may find someone a generous giver in church but a poor donor to those in immediate need. The solution applied sometimes is to pray over gifts before handing them over. Nowadays even when couples receive gifts after their weddings, the practice is to have these gifts blessed by a priest so as to ward off any debilitating occult influences.

Fear nourished by superstitious beliefs is both real and imagined.

In the Post Synodal Apostolic Exhortation of Benedict the XVl, the Holy Father observed that "Witchcraft, which is based on the traditional religions, is currently experiencing a certain revival. Old fears are re-surfacing and creating paralyzing bonds of subjection. Anxiety over health, well-being, children, the climate, and protection from evil spirits at times lead people to have recourse to practices of traditional African religions that are incompatible with Christian teaching."[9] Thus apart from the fact that families may be evolving from the extended model to the nuclear in Africa, enhanced by an economic situation which limits the financial capacity of individuals, supernatural factors may gradually be creeping in to lower levels of giving to the needy. Similarly religious influences especially in the Pentecostal folds, which maximize adherent's giving vertically to God, with the pastor as beneficiary, negatively impact on horizontal commitments by individuals to others especially people of little acquaintance.

The Lord Jesus, in the story of the Good Samaritan clearly offers a model that overcomes fear, prejudice and all hindrances towards anyone that requires help. The Samaritans were a breed of Jews. While they referred to themselves as BeneYisrael (Children of Israel), "they never referred to themselves as Yehudim (Judeans), the standard Hebrew name for Jews, considering the later to denote only mainstream Jews."[10] Samaritans believe they retained the true religion, unlike the mainstream Jewish religion believed to have been contaminated with the Babylonian exile. Their own variant of the Torah states clearly that Mount Gerizim is the place Yahweh has chosen for the building of the Temple, not Jerusalem[11]. Samaritans and mainstream Jews had a big dividing wall sustained by hatred and prejudice. As usual, great enmities sometimes arise from little differences. We see however in Scripture that Jesus made a conscious attempt to dislodge these barriers, not only through the Parable of the Good Samaritan, but by praising the Samaritan Leper who came back in thanksgiving (Lk 17:11-19), having a conversation with a Samaritan woman by the well (John 4:4-42), and in the inclusion of Samaritan territory as primary jurisdiction for the apostles' evangelizing ministry (Acts 1:8).

The Good Samaritan model therefore is one that confronts the reality with positive action. It is too spontaneous to reflect on differences and any negative consequences to self in the offer of life enhancing support to another; it universalizes brotherhood and widens the primary sphere of concern and care to include those one has never met. It is a model of self- giving, with the intended result of restoring the afflicted to a state of well- being and autonomy especially from own or self-mobilized resources.

Rich Nation, Poor People: I will never forget what an Italian lady tour guide told a group of us from Nigeria in Rome during the international retreat for priests: 'Your country is rich under but poor above.' It is a fitting capture of the paradox that is Nigeria. With huge oil and gas resources, this sector accounts for more than 35% of gross domestic product. At the presentation of the independent audit report of the Nigeria oil and gas sector between 2009 and 2011 by Ledum Mitee the chair of the Nigeria Extractive Industries Transparency Initiative (NEITI), it was discovered that the "actual direct revenue flows to the Federation Account during the period covered by the report was $133.8 billion, the revenue flows to States amounted to $1.6billion while revenue flows to other Federal Government entities such as the NDDC and Education Tax Fund (TETFUND) amounted to $3.2billion bringing the total to… earnings of $143.5billion.'[12] As recently as February 2014 there were controversies with regards to failed remittances by NNPC, with the Central Bank Governor claiming that 20 billion US was definitely not accounted for by NNPC. The figures mentioned here do not include other internally generated revenues, as well as custom duties from imported goods and services. When you convert these amounts into Naira, staggering figures emerge which could cause immediate depression.

The truth is that Nigeria is a rich country. Weak institutions, poor leadership, a culture of gratification and corruption have all combined to ensure that massive earnings have not significantly impacted on the lives of citizens in terms of stable social infrastructure and social safety nets. Attempts by various governments in the past to create poverty reduction agencies have generally been perceived by Nigerians as lacking in transparency and exclusively for the connected. While we wait for such initiatives as the conditional cash transfers to truly kick-start, whether at state or through federal agencies, the individual Nigerian must awaken to the consciousness that s/he must come down from his or her high horse and tend the hungry poor.

Get Involved, Locate and Feed the Hungry Poor

I learnt of a practice carried out by one individual, which inspired part of the title of this write up. This man made a commitment to giving what would be enough for a day's meal every day, to anyone he would judge as needing such assistance. I guess, even if this man was giving one thousand naira a day, that would amount to thirty thousand naira in a month, and up to three hundred and sixty thousand naira a year (N360,000). Rather than do nothing at all, this conscientious commitment is quite commendable.

But suppose this man decided to meet with the parish priest of a struggling parish and asked for the names of twelve struggling women whom he could assist with the sum of 30,000 each for a micro enterprise; wouldn't this be a more sustainable way of lifting people out of hunger with lasting effects? He might even decide to give N30,000 a month to one person for this purpose, in case he couldn't raise the entire 360,000 at once. Another way might be to reduce the burden of an economically challenged family by opting to train one child, this way the family could channel more resources to food, and would also potentially have a future bread winner in that child.

Apart from direct individual assistance, other ways to help might be to consistently assist such groups as St. Vincent de Paul with a reasonable amount rather than the token afterthought donations we give after mass as they clang their metallic boxes chanting 'Help the poor....Help the poor'. There is a network of these organizations tending to the ever increasing number of needy persons, such that one can never give enough. One may also decide to be part of a parish group on Justice, Development and Peace (JDPC). This group could influence larger action at parish level and even at the local government and state level when it works in collaboration with the diocesan JDPC office.

Conclusion:

In Octogessima Adveniens, Pope Paul VI talks about the victims of change. These are the 'new poor', those on the fringes, especially in our urban areas who in the elusive quest for the golden fleece have become even more dehumanized.[13] He then calls to action every Christian : *"Let each one of us examine ourselves, to see what we have done up to now, and what we ought to do. It is not enough to recall principles ,state intentions, point to crying injustice and utter prophetic denunciations; these words will lack real weight unless they are accompanied for each individual by a livelier awareness of personal responsibility and by effective action"*[14]

As a Church, traditionally, one of the key thematic approaches to issues is preferential option for the poor. This option *"affects the life of each Christian inasmuch as he or she seeks to imitate the life of Christ, but it applies equally to our social responsibilities and hence to our manner of living, and to the logical decisions to be made concerning ownership and use of goods."*[15]

The implication is that our plans and budgets must always make allowance for 'the other' or the neighbor, as our resources are not ours but given to us by God for our good and the good of others. According to John Paul ll, *"a greater responsibility rests on those who have more and can do more."*[16]

A fundamental basis of this responsibility is the affirmation, promotion and protection of human dignity, which John Paul ll sees as a debt which everyone owes[17]; this is in line with what St. Paul writes in the Letter to the Romans, "Do not owe anyone anything except to love one another, for the one who loves another has fulfilled the law."[18] Even more compelling and rewarding is the fact that it is a direct ministry to Christ Jesus himself when one serves the needy. The Lord Jesus said: "Truly I tell you, whatever you did for one of the least of these brothers and sisters of mine, you did it for me."[19]

Pope Paul Vl said in Populorum Progressio, *"Let everyone examine their conscience, a conscience that conveys a new message for our times. Are we prepared to support out of our own pocket works and undertakings organized in favour of the destitute ?"*[20] To answer this challenge positively there must be a change in lifestyles, a commitment to live simply. People pay hundreds of thousands of Naira for their children in certain schools when the child of the 'neighbour' wears a torn uniform to school. Hundreds of thousands are spent on parties when some families are not sure of a decent meal. Multiple millions are spent on furnishing, while the roof of the neighbor is leaking. We will gradually have to do injury to the sense of vanity that surrounds our dressing, our furnishings, and our accumulations and give away the outputs of our efforts to those who need them the most. The prophet Isaiah already talked about a fast that was pleasing to God: "Is it not to share your bread with the hungry, and that you bring to your house the poor who are cast out ...[21]

We will also have to find ways in which these positive actions of ours could be institutionalized, through collaboration with existing structures that the church has established to assist the poor and needy. The result will be that St. Vincent de Paul, Justice Development and Peace Committees of Parishes and Dioceses, National Lenten Appeals, will become the richer for it, for we would have inculcated a spirit of solidarity that penetrates the depths of our skin to the veins of our heart.

It is time to stop looking up to Europe or America to assist us with our poor. There are enormous resources in this country. The Bishops have established the Catholic Caritas Foundation of Nigeria to promote local giving and possibly turn the Nigerian church into a donor church where poorer nations in the subcontinent could seek support from. It is possible. As the Holy Father Benedict XVl said in Africae Munus, '*Africa is capable of providing every individual and every nation of the continent with the basic conditions which will enable them to share in development. Africans will thus be able to place their God-given talents and riches at the service of their land and their brothers and sisters.*'[22].

REFERENCES

[1] *United Nations General Assembly Outcome Document 2013*

[2]Worldometers. (2016) *Nigeria Population (1950 -2016)* [Online] Available from http://www.worldometers.info/world-population/Nigeria-population [Accessed: 11/7/2016]

[3a] AKINYELE, A. O. (2009). *Ensuring Food and Nutrition Security in Rural Nigeria: An Assessment of the Challenges, Information Needs, and Analytic Capacity.* Background paper No. NSSP 007. [Online] Available from http://www.ifpri.org/publication/ensuring-food-and-nutrition-security-rural-nigeria. [Accessed 8/11/2014]

[3b]Food Deficit of Undernourished Population. [Online] Available from hi.knoema.como/atlas/Nigeria/Food-deficit-of-undernourished-population. [Accessed 11/7/2016]

[4] The 40-Hour Famine. [Online] Available from https://40hrfamine.wordpress.com/how-hunger-hurts/ [Accessed 8/11/2014]

[5] ibid

[6]Eluaka, B.N. (2014) Nutrition Education and Counselling: Monitoring Growth and Resilience in Children. *Lenten Guide. 2014. PP 15 -31.*

[7] Turning the Tide of Nutrition: Responding to the Challenge of the 21st Century. World Health Organisation in conjunction with Nutrition for Health and Development(NHD) and Sustainable Development and Healthy Environments(SDE).[Online] Available from apps.who.int/iris/bitstream/10665/66505/1/WHO_NHD_007.pdf [Accessed on 7/11/2014] *p.3*

[8]Oxford Advanced Learner's Dictionary, S.V. Superstition, Oxford University Press, Oxford 7th Edition,2005

[9] Benedict XVI, (2011). Africae Munus. Post Synodal Apostolic Exhortation.Nairobi: Paulines Publications Africa, no.93

[10] Wikipedia.org/wiki/Samaritans

[11] ibid

[12] http://www.marineandpetroleum.com/node/80

[13] Pope Paul Vl (1990).On New Social Problems. Nairobi: Paulines Publications Africa, no.15

[14] Ibid no.48.

[15] John Paul ll, (1987). On Social Concern. Nairobi: Paulines Publication Africa, no.42.

[16] Ibid no.47.

[17] Ibid no.47

[18]International Standard Version Bible

[19] Matt. 25:40.

[20] Pope Paul, (1990). On the Development of Peoples. Nairobi: Paulines Publications Africa, no.47

[21]Isaiah 58:7

1. [22] *No 24*

CHAPTER TWO

GOOD GOVERNANCE: EXPLORING THE ECCLESIAL CONSTITUENCY

INTRODUCTION: In Owerri, capital of Imo State, during the military era, the military administrator summoned the Archbishop of Owerri, Anthony Obinna. The Archbishop was reported to have said something critical of his administration so he wanted the Archbishop to come and explain. The Archbishop announced in Church that he had been summoned by the Military Administrator and that he would be going on foot to meet up the appointment and wanted his flock to escort him. At the appointed time, crowds of people turned out to accompany him to government house. However along the way, news must have gotten to the Military Administrator about the hoard of people massing towards his office for he quickly sent emissaries to cancel the summons.

This was a classic example of cultivating the ecclesial community to confront high handedness of those in authority. The thesis is well known that where the people properly and consistently mobilise themselves and stand together against an issue, guns or tyrants would budge. There have been many cases where peoples' power caused change. The most recent have been the Arab Springs which have raised questions of how those societies were governed, leading to new constitutions and new peoples' deals. Soldiers in Russia could not shoot their guns at the sight of masses of people, the guards by the Berlin Wall could not restrain the crowd that surged, which eventually broke the dichotomy between East and

West Germany; and many years ago, in 1986 to be precise, the Church mobilized the people in a bloodless revolution, to bring down a corrupt government in the Philippines. It might be worth taking a look, even if it is a cursory one, at the situation that existed then in the Philippines.

The Philippines Snap Elections

America is traditionally an ally of the Philippines and as expected was solidly behind the government of Fidel Marcos. But there was growing discontent with his administration, especially with the death of Benigno Aquino who was gruesomely murdered. To strengthen his hold on power and reaffirm to his people that he still had legitimacy as well as enormous goodwill from the American people, Marcos decided for an earlier election. One year into the expiry of his six year tenure, the election held. Meanwhile the Archbishop of Manilla, Cardinal Sin, convinced the two major opposition leaders to team up and confront the incumbent, with Laurel therefore ceding the presidential slot to Aquino's widow and becoming her vice. Cardinal Sin knew that the ruling party would bribe the people to vote for them and traditionally they were obliged to do so once receiving a bribe, he therefore went onto the church run radio network and advised that an immoral contract was not binding and therefore people should vote according to their consciences. The people voted *en mass* for Aquino-Laurel ticket but the results were declared in favour of the incumbent. It was so obvious that the elections were rigged. It began with two top military commanders rebelling against Marcos and asking him to resign. They set up their rebel camps with troops loyal to them. Markos's order that loyal troops engage rebel troops and suppress the uprising was again contained by Cardinal Sin who urged the people on the catholic radio network, Veritas, to turn out with food for the rebel soldiers and form a shield around them. Hundreds of thousands of people turned out, including priests and religious. In the face of such a sea of people, some loyal troops defected including some of those with helicopter gunships who were to fire against the troops and possibly the people. After an inauguration which had only the newly appointed Soviet Ambassador present, Marcos was advised by a US Senator to quit, as he was no longer under the protection of the United States.[1] Marcos ran away to the United States shortly afterwards.

Dissecting the Church's Role

Examining the above scenario three main things stand out: An influential cleric, the existence of an independent medium of mass communication and the moral will to stand by the people against the establishment. Cardinal Sin was obviously an astute cleric with great political sense. Being at the nation's capital he had national acclaim in a country that had its majority citizens as Catholic, including the president of the country. His sphere of influence was enormous. Nigeria is a country that is probably divided equally between the two religions, with Catholics being about 30 million out of a population of 177 million. While many clerics are quite well known for their prophetic roles at state, regional and national levels, nevertheless, a few clerics stand out whose names are known by virtually all Nigerians. In most dioceses within the country, clerics are respected by the people and by civil authorities.

However the complexity of the political landscape in Nigeria, including religion, and ethnic configuration make it a tough task to have complete consensus and a single figure as a rallying point; it becomes a challenge therefore to harness the entire potential of the leverage every cleric could have, nationally. Nigeria is home to more than 350 ethnic groups.

In terms of means of communication, although there is the liberalization of licenses with regards to communications media, there is still a hold on exclusively religious stations.[2] Nevertheless broadcast opportunities are provided by various independent networks, most especially Africa Independent Television(AIT). But this may not achieve such an aim as achieved in the Philippines.

The Catholic Bishops Conference of Nigeria have consistently been pro people and pro poor in their many communiqués after their plenary meetings. With the presidency of Archbishop Ignatius Kaigama, a new dynamism has been brought to bear, where the Bishops do not need to wait to hold their statutory meetings before responding to issues of national importance. Using Skype and teleconferencing, the Bishops' position on issues has been defined and proclaimed. For instance during the Ebola crises, during the debate on capital punishment; Bishops themselves have engaged in face to face meetings with the President of the Federal Republic, with regards the state of insecurity and the malaise of the internally displaced persons.

The question is, is there still more that could be done to make the church more politically relevant, or more on the side of the people ? The answer is yes, and it lies in the very shepherd role of the cleric.

The Cleric as Leader

When we talk of the cleric as leader, we are not referring to the kind of authority the Lord Jesus condemned when he said "You know that the rulers of the Gentiles lord it over them, and their high officials exercise authority over them…"(Matthew 20:25). Rather Jesus admonished: "Not so with you. Instead, whoever wants to become great among you must be your servant."(v.26).

This kind of notion accommodates such other notions of leadership as accompaniment, as when Lao Tsu the Chinese philosopher says "To lead people, walk beside them. As for the best leaders, the people do not notice their existence…When the best leader's work is done, the people say, 'We did it ourselves'"

By the very fact that most clerics are placed in charge of people, they are leaders. They accompany their flock, they are there when they are initiated into the church, they are there when they marry, they are there when they are sick, they are there when they die; they are there to listen and advise.

How could clerics turn this enormous potential into real influence ?

I want to suggest a few points.

Realizing his enormous power: Unfortunately the word power has been corrupted in its understanding to be associated with mean egocentricism. 'The man likes power' can mean a man is autocratic, unaccommodating, even repressive. But I love the simple definition given by Ed Chambers, one of the leaders of the Industrial Areas Foundation. According to him "power is ability to act." With this understanding power is seen in a more comprehensive and inclusive sense, and not something exclusive to certain individuals. "Like the capacity to love, it is given to us at birth. Power is our birthright, our inheritance."[3] Chambers laments the English understanding of the word which is mostly seen as a noun and unilateral. Says he "English speakers not only misunderstand power as a noun, as something that can be possessed and used at will as an instrument, but also assume that it exists in a fixed quantity. Just as there is only so much gold in the world, there is only so much power to go around. If I get some more, you lose it… But power is not zero sum."[4] Thus power would have more meaning not as a noun but as a verb eg to be able to influence and be influenced, to be able to give and take, to be able to persuade etc. To have power would mean having a certain capacity. This is not strange to Spanish speakers who often use *podes – to be able.* The cleric must therefore realize his tremendous capacity to influence, to negotiate, to lead.

From Politics to Politicalness: The cleric should realize how politically relevant his position is, as far as he is a leader of people. Unfortunately politics is seen as a dirty game. I once asked a group of children how many of them would want to be politicians and none agreed to, saying politicians were thieves, liars, fraudsters etc. But when I asked how many wanted to be governor they all raised their hands. Because of the strong association of politics with something negative, as if it were the prerogative of those seeking political office, some scholars are of the view that we use politicalness instead of simply politics. "By politicalness I mean our capacity for developing into beings who know and value what it means to participate in and be responsible for the care and improvement of our common and collective life."[5]

Catholic Social Teaching emphasizes this element of participation. In other words the cleric cannot be aloof, facing only the spiritual aspects of the life of the people without realizing the complementarity of other aspects and the ability of one to impinge on others. Misuse of political office for instance is deprivative of resources for the common good, with attendant consequences of poverty, poor infrastructure, poor access to social services. We could therefore borrow an Aristotelian model of citizenship which he saw as of necessity inclusive of participation in the affairs of the city state. In fact the reason Aristotle called man a 'political animal was because 'we cannot be fully human without participation in a city-state.'[6] If politics is seen in this sense of politicalness, then we are going to see working for the common good as a collective responsibility and place value in educating our people to know their worth and have a voice to express themselves on issues affecting them and actually influence those issues.

Emphasizing an Aspect of Leadership: It is usually taken for granted that anyone in a position of authority is a leader. This is true, as we have acknowledged earlier. However it might be good to stretch this understanding a bit. Advocacy groups do not see the leader as an individual, they see him/her as a representative of a constituency. A parish priest for instance is a leader because he can act on behalf of his parishioners, because even if he stands alone it is presumed that his parishioners are behind him. In other words the leader must have such leverage as to be able to deliver his constituency when the need arises. The Industrial Areas Foundation therefore see a leader as one with a following that could be delivered.[7] In this sense the Archbishop who had masses of people following him to the Military Administrator's summons is a leader, the Cardinal who turned out hundreds of thousands of people through his appeal, is a leader. If those who are supposed to take the instruction or respond to the appeal or invitation of someone in authority turn out not to do so, and for no cause as such, the one in authority is not seen as a leader; according to the understanding of these groups, he is only occupying a position. A point to meditate here is how much effort we put into promoting a cause or an event and how much participants identify with it and own it. The salient realization is that the leader must always look out for what is of common interest and how his flock's personal or self interest(not selfish interest) is captured in the common interest so that there is broad based ownership.

Archbishop Obinna and the Leverage of Power: In the 2015 electoral campaigns, both presidential candidates of All Progressives Congress(APC) and Peoples Democratic Party(PDP) visited the Archbishop of Owerri in his official residence. That is, the president of the Federal Republic of Nigeria and General Muhammadu Buhari paid courtesy visits to the Archbishop of Owerri to seek his support. Why did they do this ? Because every politician has now come to understand that if you want to succeed in Imo State, you wouldn't ignore the Archbishop of Owerri who calls the shots among the Catholic population, who by the way are in the majority. It means he had risen to a point he could not be ignored, a point of respect. Apart from the civil respect to the clergy generally, respect in this sense comes from leverage, that is, the level of influence the church could have in making or marring the ambition or policies of political office holders, and such leverage only comes from certain tensions in the relationship of power which resolved favourably to the one with the leverage. Ikedi Ohakim lost his second term bid because the church mobilized against him, so any politician would be wary of such leverage.

The leader of a flock cannot therefore abdicate his duty of politicalness. He has to organize his flock to have this leverage and be wary of acts that could undermine this leverage for example personal gifts from political office holders; as Goethe said, 'If you eat my bread, you sing my song.' Rather he would direct gifts to service or charitable institutions and make sure the office holder is aware of this, if he cannot reject them altogether.

Just A Few Questions: I will pose a few questions and if the answer is no then the leader knows he has a lot of grounds to cover. As a parish priest, does your local government chairman know you ? If he knows you, is it as the priest who usually comes around to invite him to the harvest or as one who speaks about a need in a community ? (A priest in a very poor parish rejected cash from the local government chairman and told him to use it to fix the borehole in the community). Would the office holder pick your call or return it if he missed it ? When it is time for elections do political office aspirants inform you of their intention and seek your support ? During the budget process do they ask for your input, and would they accept an input from you ? When you request for a meeting does the political office holder take it as a priority and attend by him/herself or does s/he delegate a non-descript official or completely ignore your request ? Can you and your parishioners influence the outcome of an election without appearing partisan ?

The wider one's jurisdiction, the wider the potential sphere of influence. For instance a Bishop's influence would then depend on the aggregate of leverages the parishes can muster.

Conclusion:

This is not a call to be involved in partisan politics. The point here rather is that as citizens those who lead should learn the dynamics of that position and use it for the good of the people, especially in a context where the politician feels insulated and supreme, towering above the sovereignty of the people. Leaders must take seriously the civic education of their flock and organize them to be conscious of their political capital. In doing this they should collaborate with like structures, for instance in a geographical area Catholic, Protestant and Muslim clergy should form a local coalition which regularly assesses the social condition of their flock which they bring to the attention of government at the various levels. As John Paul ll said in Sollicitudo Rei Socialis, "The obligation to commit oneself to the development of peoples is not just an individual duty…it is an imperative which obliges each and every man and woman, as well as societies and nations. In particular, it obliges the Catholic Church and the other Churches and Ecclesial Communities , with which we are completely willing to collaborate in this field."[8] United action on behalf of the people is the best option than singular or isolated efforts.

They should organize as well the resources within the community so that the community is not dependent on resources that come from government for needs which are exclusively ecclesial in their nature; rather they should use their leverage to advocate for greater access for the entire community to infrastructure that meet the social needs. If the clergy put their act together and focus more on the interest of their flock, they would be in a position to lead their people to engage government to be more accountable and transparent and therefore meeting the needs of the people. And what else is good governance ?

REFERENCES

1. www.country-data.com/cgi.../r-10408.ht...
2. Section 10 of Decree no.38 of 1992 bans broadcast houses for political parties and religious groups.
3. Edward Chambers with Michael Cowen, *Roots for Radicals: Organisng for Power,Action and Justice*, (New York: The Continuum International Publishing Group, 2003),p.27
4. Chambers, p.28
5. Sheldon Wolin, *The Presence of the Past* (Baltimore:johns Hopkins University Press, 1989), p.139.
6. http://.m.sparknotes.com/.../Aristotle/section10...
7. Edward Chambers,p,51.
   John Paul ll, *Solicitudo Rei Socialis* (Nairobi: Paulines Publications Africa, 2001), no.32

CHAPTER THREE

BOKO HARAM TERRORISM AND NATIONAL COHESION IN NIGERIA: ISSSUES IN NIGERIAN NATIONAL IDENTITY

1.1 The objective of this paper is to make an expose on the national identity crisis in Nigeria and how Boko Haram terrorism has deconstructed this crisis. The paper suggests that an opportunity exists to construct a Nigerian identity through the bonding made possible by the threat of terrorism.

1.2 Geographically, Nigeria is situated in West Africa. The last population census conducted in Nigeria was in 2006, putting Nigeria at a little over 140 million persons. However current estimates made in 2014 and published by the Nigeria Bureau of Statistics put Nigeria at 178.5 million inhabitants.[1]

1.3 Nigeria has more than two hundred and fifty ethnic nationalities, each speaking a different language. English serves as the official language, effectively providing a means of communication among the various ethnic groups who otherwise would not have been able to communicate effectively.   Three major ethnic groupings stand out: the Hausa-Fulani, the Yorubas and the Igbos. The Hausa –Fulani are found mostly in the northern part of the country while the Yorubas occupy largely the South West and the Igbos the South East.

1.3.1 Nigerians are almost evenly distributed among the two major religions of Christianity and Islam. However traditional religious adherents still exist in many parts of Nigeria. The traditional religion and customs are still part of the religious and cultural psyche of the average Nigerian who still resorts to certain superstitious beliefs despite conversion to Christianity or Islam. Many leaders of indigenous Christian sects have adapted certain syncretic practices which incorporate aspects of traditional belief systems.

1.4 Politically Nigeria is a republic, practicing the American type of Presidential democracy. After gaining independence from British colonial rule in1960 and being a republic in 1963, the military took over power in 1966 and supervised a civil war which lasted for three years, from 1967 to 1970. The military handed back power to civilians in 1978 and the second republic was cut short in 1983 by Muhammadu Buhari a then military general. It wasn't until 1999 that the third republic was established with the handing over of power to a former military head of state, Olusegun Obasanjo. Since 1999 Nigeria has held elections successfully for five times, with successful transitions to new governments. The most successful of the transitions was the hand over of power from an incumbent government of President Goodluck Jonathan to Muhammadu Buhari the All Progressive Congress Party candidate who won the keenly contested presidential elections in April 2015.

2.0 National Identity Issues in Nigeria

National identity is "the sense of a nation as a cohesive whole, as represented by distinctive traditions, culture, language and politics. A person's national identity is his/her identity and sense of belonging to one state or to one nation, a feeling one shares with a group of people, regardless of one's legal citizenship status."[2]

 When individual citizens, and as groups buy into a sense of cohesiveness and own it, it is expressed in patriotism, which is the best expression of national identity. The opposite is ethnic, regional or religious chauvinism.

Political writers like Francis Fukayama have touched on issues of national identity in Nigeria. According to Fukayama (Fukayama, 2014 p.(225)) in his latest book entitled ***Political Order and Political Decay,*** "The Nigerian State is weak not only in technical capacity and its ability to enforce laws impersonally and transparently. It is also weak in a moral sense. It has a deficit of legitimacy. There is little loyalty to a nation called Nigeria that supersedes ties to one's region, ethnic group, or religious community. The country's complex electoral laws require that a president be elected not just by a plurality of votes in a national election, but that he or she receive a certain number of votes in different regions of the country...But it does not guarantee that Nigerians will feel a common sense of national identity, or that they will trust the president and other national leaders to treat their group fairly."[3]

Fukayama sums up aptly the effects of an absence of national identity, which is a loss of the sense of the common good and in its stead the pursuit of individual and regional agenda. Many factors may have contributed to this situation.

2.1 The Amalgamation of the North and South that took place in 1914 by the British Colonialists seems to have been a forced marriage. The British used the Indirect Rule system in the North, using the existing political structures they met on ground to govern the people. Having been conquered by Uthman Dan Fodio through a jihad that spread across most of the North East and North West, Northern Nigeria had a system of emirs ruling over the people, combining religious authority and political authority. Southern Nigeria had a mix of systems depending on the area: the Yorubas had their system of Obas, while the Igbos were more municipal and republican. Other ethnic groups had their systems of chiefdoms as well. The Royal Niger Company through effective trade, had established a system of ruling directly over the people until direct colonial administrations were set up. In terms of language, politics, culture, religion, there was not much identity between the North and South. While most of the South became Christian, the core North remained principally muslim. Till date many Nigerian writers and commentators still go back to 1914 to identify it as a marriage of inconvenience.

2.2 The civil war fought between 1967 and 1970 is another factor. Before the civil war the sense of ethnic identity was not conflicting with national identity. Nigerians could live freely anywhere and own property without fear of losing it one day. However a military coup in 1966 led by officers of Igbo extraction managed to eliminate largely Northern officers. The seeds of discord were sown when Northern officers staged a counter coup six months later and eliminated officers of Eastern origin, including the then military head of state, General Aguiyi Ironsi. Ironsi it was who introduced a unitary system from the regional con-federal government that existed. Since the coup and counter-coup, ethnic animosity grew in leaps and bounds, leading finally to a declaration of secession by the Eastern region led by Lt. Col Odumegwu Ojukwu. The attempt to quell the secession led to the civil war which lasted for three years. Although no Victor nor Vanquished was declared, the sense of bonding as a nation was further disintegrated with the experience of the war. Not only was the core North an enemy of the East, the South-West too were joined in because of the perceived role of certain actors before and during the war who were from the region notably Obafemi Awolowo whose policies crippled Biafra and fast tracked the end of the war. The minority groups in the Eastern region began to have a sense of ethnic identity as opposed to a national identity because they started feeling that the majority Igbo group were only interested in their own advancement and not factoring in the needs of the minorities, even as the emerging oil wealth was in the vicinities of the minority groups.

2.3 Power sharing became a contributory factor to the crisis of national identity. Since the North took power through the military in 1966, power only went back to the South in 1976 after the assassination of General Murtala Muhammad. Olusegun Obasanjo, a Yoruba from the South West, handed over power voluntarily to the civilian regime of Alhaji Shehu Shagari from the North. Shagari was overthrown after four and a half years by General Muhammadu Buhari, a Northerner who was overthrown in 1985 by another Northerner, General Babangida. Babangida ruled for eight years, conducted an election which was adjudged the freest and fairest in the nation's history, won by a South-Westerner, Moshood Abiola, a multi-Billionaire. But the elections were annulled, which pitched the South-West against the North. An interim government was formed headed by Ernest Shonekan a man from the South-West, about six months later this administration was set aside by General Sanni Abacha, a northerner. He ruled from November 1993 till his death in 1998. General Abdulsalami Abubakar, a northerner took over from him and handed over to an elected administration of General Olusegun Obasanjo, a South-Westerner. He in turn handed over power after eight years to Musa Y'Ardua, a northerner, who died in office two and a half years into his tenure. Goodluck Jonathan, his vice, a minority from the oil producing Niger Delta, took over and two years later contested and won his first election as president. He governed in those fours years amidst heavy threats of the Boko Haram terrorism. It was the first time that someone from a minority group would accede the presidency. He lost the 2015 elections to a Northerner, Muhammadu Buhari, who was taking another shot at being at the helm of affairs after nearly thirty years. Goodluck Jonathan lost mostly because the North felt it was it's turn to take back the presidency after a stint by the late Y'Ardua. There is thus an ingrained resentment of southern groups especially minority groups who feel the north believes it has a right to rule. Many people have made proposals about entrenching zoning into the constitution to allow for the participation of all groups in sharing power.

2.4 Another strong factor against national identity is the indigene-settler issue. This connects with the power access issue above as well. In Nigeria one's native community matters so much, that even when one's grandfather migrated and settled somewhere else, the grandchildren are still not seen as indigenes of where their grandfather settled; they are regarded as settlers. Although taxes are collected from the 'settler' as s/he probably was born, lives and works there, s/he may still not access certain benefits. Nigeria has 774 Local Government Areas. Each of these local government areas issues a certificate of origin "which identify a person as an indigene of a particular locality. Accessing land, schools, civil service jobs, or public office without one can be almost impossible....Bona fide applicants are turned away because of their religion and appearance, or handed papers solely on those grounds. Often the process becomes a toll-keeping exercise, in which corrupt officials christen anyone who pays a bribe an indigene."[4] Perhaps issuing this certificate as part of a process of birth registration, if at all this certificate of origin is relevant, might be a way to contain issues arising from it for future generations.

2.5 The perception of access to oil wealth is a major issue contributing to the national identity crisis. During the reign of General Abacha, in his attempt to transit into a civilian president, he organized a million man march which brought youths from the Niger Delta to Abuja, Nigeria's political capital for the first time. The evidence of infrastructure and opulence at display in the capital, as contrasted with the poor state of affairs in the oil producing Niger Delta, led to the rise of insurgency in the Niger Delta. Attacks on oil facilities, kidnap of oil workers, amounted to an economic sabotage which spiraled the price of oil around the world. The perception that the goose that lays the golden egg was not well fed, led to resentment against the Northern ruling elite, who were perceived to acquire most of the oil blocks. Aside military solutions to combat the militancy in the Niger Delta, an Amnesty program which reintegrated the militants into society by training them in skills and businesses was established. The threat to end the amnesty program, in spite of perceived massive fraud has caused the erstwhile militant leaders to regroup with real threat to national security. The Avengers easily come to mind.

2.6 The greatest threat to national identity is perhaps the avarice nature of Nigerian politics. Nigeria is one of the most corrupt nations on earth. Acording to Transparency International, Nigeria currently ranks as the 39th most corrupt country [5]. Occupying an elective or politically appointive position is the easiest way to personal wealth in Nigeria. The common wealth is regarded as 'personal' estate. Such positions as governor, President, have immunity from prosecution while in office. The monthly security vote which runs into millions of naira which is not publicly accountable is an automatic savings for governors. From the lowest political office of Councilor to the highest offices, election is a capital intensive contestation, many times leading to violent loss of lives. The ordinary Nigerian sees the crass opportunism and the corruption among office holders and knows that there is nothing patriotic about political office in Nigeria, that every office is for personal enrichment and to assuage the rent seeking supporters; that there is the gross lack of a sense of sacrifice and service which is essential for any development of patriotic instincts.

2.7 A consequence of corruption is that rather than develop infrastructure and create social safety nets, the Nigerian state becomes quite weak and incapable of meeting the most basic provisions for her citizens such as housing, water and sanitation, energy for both domestic and industrial usage. The poor become quite vulnerable, without being able to care even for health needs. The National Health Act was an attempt to make health access a right, but this is limited to the federal government, as states are not bound except the Act is domesticated within their states. The average Nigerian thus believes the state owes him/her nothing, and so s/he in turn owes the state nothing. The over dependence on oil revenue for government running, rather than on citizen taxation created a mutually laisser-faire attitude between officials of state and citizens, as state officials plundered unhindered the revenues from oil and the citizen was happy to go about his/her business without any real tax obligation.

The effect of all these factors on the average Nigerian psyche has been a loss of faith in the nation called Nigeria and the accentuation of communal and tribal identities. John Campbell says "Nigerian political life is based on patronage-clientage networks, and religious and ethnic loyalties supersede those to the nation."[6]

3.0 Boko Haram and National Identity

It is a truism that whenever a nation faces an external threat, the citizens are united in facing it. It was speculated for instance that George W. Bush Jnr would have lost his second term bid as president of the United States but for the September 9/11 attacks which galvanized the whole nation against the Al Qaeda threat and inadvertently secured his victory at the polls, because though they saw him as a bad manager of the economy and even going into a needless war against Iraq, a measure of confidence was reposed on him in facing up to external threats. This may have worked similarly with the Boko Haram threat, except in reverse, as citizens of Nigeria saw the erstwhile President Goodluck Ebele Jonathan as incapable of confronting the threat to the corporate existence of Nigeria and voted him out in April 2015.

3.1 Boko Haram was begun by Mohammed Yusuf as a simple sect of Islam in Maiduguri, Borno State . It is not uncommon in Northern Nigeria to have religious leaders establish sects. Yusuf established a centre with a mosque and an Islamic school for boys, with boarding facilities. His line of doctrine was the radical Wahhabi teaching which subscribes to a very strict monotheism and sees the secularity of the state, with its attendant anthems, flags and symbols as idolatrous. These also include anything western, especially western education. Embracing a violent jihadi approach meant that it is a Salafi movement as well. "Salafism is a call for a return to the beliefs, practices, and sincerity of early Islam. In fact the term Salafism is a direct reference to these early years, and refers to the first few generations of Muslims, known as *salaf.*"[7](Stern, J. Berger J.M. ,p.(263)). The Salafis got radicalized into a violent jihadi angle during the Soviet invasion of Afghanistan and gradually concretized the notion that a violent approach could better advance the interests of the muslim world.[8](p.268). This meant that Boko Haram would see those who did not subscribe to their kind of Islam as corrupt and even non-muslims, and therefore any means in their elimination was legitimate. In 1982 Abd al Salam Faraj popularized the notion of jihad "as second only to belief" in his pamphlet The Neglected Duty, and argued that the declaration of jihad did not require a central authority like the state. Salafi groups like Boko Haram and ISIS thus subscribe to this very decentralized autorising of jihad, making violent jihad equal to Islam itself.[9](p.272).   Obviously Yusuf thoroughly indoctrinated his pupils with this Wahhabi-Salafi doctrine. Security forces began to keep an eye on the group, as Northern Nigeria is known for religious riots. Some sources say that it was the security forces that instigated the violence of the group. Obviusly with their salafist jihadi orientation, there was going to be violence eventually anyway, but the trigger seemed to be when Boko Haram members were going to bury their dead member and were confronted by the police; an encounter ensued which led to the death of a member. Consequently Boko Haram organized a coordinated revenge in several cities which saw to the death of more than 100 persons within a matter of days. Members were rounded up, including their leader. The death of Muhammad Yusuf under police custody, was the melting point of aggression. But the group disbanded temporarily, went into alliances that saw to the building of their capacity in guerilla warfare, bomb making and all such terrorist activities and resurfaced in 2009.

The accentuation of their attacks coincided with the accession to the presidency of Goodluck Jonathan after his election; it therefore gave the impression that the Muslim North was using a military arm to destabilize the government of a Southern minority President. For months and years this was the narrative, which prevented government from confronting it as a national threat. The initial terrorism of Boko Haram, especially with their attacks on churches polarized the nation and fatally damaged any national cohesion, although they did not succeed in instigating retaliation from Christians, which would have led to a religious war. But suspicion and fear of Muslims just because they dressed and prayed in a certain way, gained enormous grounds. The silence of the northern Muslim elite further fuelled the speculation that Boko Haram was a northern Muslim political agenda. This political perception overshadowed the quest to unmask it for what it really was, Islamic fundamentalism seeking to establish a theocracy. It was when Boko Haram spread its attacks to Muslims as well and evolved all forms of elusive tactics that Nigerians began to realize that this was indeed a national and not a regional threat, and began to rally around their national identity. But majority of Nigerians had lost confidence in the ability of Goodluck Jonathan, immediate past president, because they perceived him as weak. Nigerians wanted a stronger man who could lead the way in the fight for the preservation of the corporate existence of Nigeria.

This anxiety coincided with the period of the preparations towards the general elections. Apart from the internal conflicts that were inherent in the ruling Peoples' Democratic Party, the handling of the insecurity by the government was seen as poor. Boko Haram became emboldened by the day and actually carved out a territory within Nigeria equal to the size of Belgium. In spite of the declaration of a state of emergency in Borno, Yobe and Adamawa

States, Nigerian soldiers could not rout Boko Haram. One of the most dastardly acts of Boko Haram was the abduction of more than 200 girls from a secondary school in Chibok, Borno State. With the international outcry that greeted this event, the government of Goodluck Jonathan came under severe pressure to deal decisively with the issue of insecurity. In the wake of this abduction many foreign nations offered to support Nigeria. However not much was heard about their support. The United States for some reason was a major opponent to Nigeria acquiring sophisticated arms to deal with the terrorists.

The billions of Naira voted for security did not have any demonstrable impact as the funds were diverted possibly for personal aggrandizement while soldiers privately complained of a lack of equipment to match up with Boko Haram. This welled up a resentment in Nigerians against a robustly corrupt regime, that led to its ouster eventually through the ballot.

It must be noted however that six weeks to the general elections, the Nigerian government managed to secure sophisticated arms and through a multi-national agreement with Nigeria's neighbours that gave them the right to pursue, the Nigerian military and especially with the support of the Chadian military, were able to annex all the territories of Boko Haram including their headquarters. This did not however stop the defeat of the incumbent in the general elections; for Nigerians then started wondering how come it was that for nearly six years Boko Haram remained undefeated but in just under six weeks all occupied territories were taken back from Boko Haram.

4.0 Conclusion

The defeat of Goodluck Ebele Jonathan, an incumbent president, with all the arsenal of presidential power in Nigeria at his disposal proves a thesis that Nigerians could forego tribal, religious and even economic differences to unite towards a national cause. Though the government of Goodluck Jonathan may have made impressive strides in other flanks, these were not noticeable to the generality of the populace, as the security threat posed by Boko Haram became the overriding issue. Nigerians saw a common enemy in Boko Haram and all wished it could be tackled to preserve Nigeria's corporate existence.

This has shown that Nigerians are not indifferent to the corporate existence of Nigeria and therefore have a form of identification with her. The election of the All Progressive Congress candidate on the platform of change, with many southern Nigerians voting for a presidential candidate from the north, showed that Nigerians desire genuine leadership, and genuine leadership could lead to a reinstatement of faith in the nation and personal identification with the aspirations of the nation irrespective of one's ethnic or cultural orientation.

Boko Haram may thus have assisted in the growing of these national identity sentiments.

REFERENCES

[1]COUNTRY METERS. *Nigeria Population Clock.*   [Online] Available from www.countrymeters.info/en/Nigeria [Accessed 13th July 2015]

[2] SEARCH WIKIPEDIA. *National Identity.* [Online]. Available from https://en.m.wikipedia.org/wiki/National_identity). [Accessed 11th July 2015]

[3]FUKAYAMA, F.(2014) *Political Order and Political Decay.* London: Profile Books. p.225

[4]SAYNE, A. *Rethinking Nigeria's Indigene-Settler Conflicts.* [Online]. Available from www.usip.org/sites/default/.../SR311.pdf p.3

[5] TRANSPARENCY INTERNATIONAL. *2014 Corruption Perception Index Measures the Perceived Levels of Public Sector*

Corruption in 175 Countries and Territories. #CPI2014.[Online]. Available from http://www.transparency.org/cpi2014. [Accessed on 13th July 2015].

[6] CAMPBELL,J. (2014) *Boko Haram: origins, challenges and responses*. Norwegian Peacebuilding Resource Centre [Online] October 2014 . Available from www.peacebuilding.no/.../original/.../... [Access 13th July 2015] p.1

[7] STERN,J. BERGER, J.M.(2015) *ISIS The State of Terror*. London:William Collins. P263

[8] STERN,J. BERGER,J.M. (2015) p.268

[9] (STERN, J. BERGER,J. M. (2015) p.272

CHAPTER FOUR

THE NIGERIAN FAMILY AND POVERTY

Introduction

Nigeria is the largest nation in Africa in terms of population. Currently she has about 177 million persons, based on the projections made by the Nigeria Census Bureau for 2014.[1] Nigeria has a total geographical area of 910,771 sq km and a total area of 923,768sq km.

Nigeria's economy was rebased in 2014 to become the largest economy on the African continent. With a growth rate that was put at 7% for nearly a decade powered by telecommunications and retail outlets, the oil percentage volume of the economy shrunk to 14%, although up till 2014 oil still accounted for up to 80% of foreign exchange earnings.[2]

The recent crash in oil prices has had devastating effect on the Nigerian economy, with an increased inability to earn foreign exchange and the consequent pressure on external reserves, on an import dependent economy. The effect on the nation's currency, the Naira has been crushing, with the Central Bank forced to devalue the Naira in December 2014 by 8.38 per cent in real terms.[3]   Since then the Naira has continued to crash in spite of efforts by the Central Bank. The dollar currently exchanges for 2008 Naira as against the 160 it was exchanging for as late as October 2014. The downfall of the Naira makes it easier for foreign investors, such that Nigeria is currently being top-rated as a frontier market by the Frontier Market Sentiment Index ; of course frontier markets are only a prelude to emerging markets.[4]

Challenges

As Nigeria carries out the four year ritual of elections early in 2015, the new government in an American styled presidential system, running uninterruptedly for 16 years, will have to contend with the full impact of the shortage of foreign earnings in an import dependent economy. Apart from the already high unemployment rate, many families will be bereft of bread winners, as government earns less and shares less to the 36 federating units and the 774 Local Government Areas which are highly dependent on the centre for oil revenue that is shared monthly; this would mean downsizing of the labour force, less investment in infrastructure and therefore less business for construction companies which employ a teeming workforce. The ripple effects on the Nigerian family could only be imagined.

The insecurity in the North East of Nigeria has spread a general climate of fear and displaced hundreds of thousands of families. "On 1st December 2014, at the Humanitarian Country Forum, the National Emergency Management Agency(NEMA), released statistics of internally displaced persons in the three State-of-Emergency states of Borno, Adamawa and Yobe. While Bornu State had 402,810 internally displaced persons, Adamawa had 160,198 and Yobe 116,538. These were persons identified in various camps, as a result of the terrorist action of Boko Haram. These statistics do not include the displaced persons as a result of the Fulani cattlemen invasion of communities in Plateau, Nassarawa, Tarabba, and parts of Benue State."[5] Nor do they include those in households in neighbouring secure towns and villages, households suddenly expanding sometimes up to 28 persons in a house that would normally accommodate 8 or so persons.[6] Never at any time in history have some Nigerian families witnessed so much displacements from their stable means of livelihood.

A silent challenge to the Nigerian family is grappling with the demands of household size. In the Muslim North, where it is part of the culture to have many wives, and where the rate of divorce is higher, family size can be between 15 to as large as 25. In the North West and North East, this leads to a phenomenon of the *Almajiri*, where parents give out their children at very tender ages to be under the tutelage of Islamic scholars; these children are sent out to beg for their livelihood as the Franciscan mendicants used to do. Many of these children have access only to Quranic education and have no exposure to skills and other forms of education that could enhance their economic situation. These children too become ready tools in the hands of politicians who may exploit their dependency for selfish political purposes not precluding violence. In large cities finding suitable accommodation for even an average family could be a challenge; in Lagos for instance a family of 7 could get cramped in one room apartments called "Face Me, Face You" because whole families squeeze into 7-by-11-foot rooms along a narrow corridor. Up to 50 people share a kitchen, toilet and sink — though the pipes in the neighborhood often no longer carry water."[7]

The rapidly growing population in Nigeria has given impetus to organisations that promote reproductive health issues bordering on contraception and abortifacients to align with government to proliferate so called family planning services in Nigeria. At primary health care level, access is granted to Nigerian women to 'plan' their families often free of charge. This is a challenge the average Catholic faces, that as much as the artificial methods are available, not much access is there for those who want to control family size through natural methods. In early 2014 Caritas Nigeria supported a meeting with the Federal Ministry of Health for the updating and inclusion of all forms of natural family planning methods in the national policy. An outcome of this was that a manual is being written for the training of medical personnel which the Federal Ministry has requested the Catholic Church to develop. Countering the offensive of the promoters of a culture of death with forms of life will continue to be a challenge as this kind of intervention remains a priority with little or no budgetary backing in the Nigerian Church, in the face of the infrastructure challenges faced by the Church in Nigeria.

A significant challenge that young people also face in Nigeria is the high rate of Catholics who are not in full communion because of marital status. This in itself has economic undertones. In 2013, precisely May, 420 Nigerian youths were interviewed nationwide by Caritas Nigeria in a survey that had to do with the best world possible. 67% identified small businesses or self employment as their main source of livelihood. 74 % identified finance and corruption as single most important constraints to their progress in life; 44% believed that tackling corruption was the single most important action that needed to be taken while 91% believed an honest and responsive government is what was needed.

 This information is important because while many young men and women may be committed to settling down to building a family, one of the main constraints is economic. Custom and tradition put barriers which only economic opportunities could surmount. For instance in many countries of Africa a sacramental wedding is preceded by an equally expensive traditional and customary wedding. This situation leaves many young people to marry late or engage in 'para-marriages' before the actual ceremonies years later, and in the meantime, they cease to be in full communion.

 With a minimum wage of less than 100 dollars a month, the average Nigerian man finds it extremely challenging to meet up with the demands of these traditional rites which are a prelude to a 'white wedding'. What therefore happens is that many people begin families by impregnating the lady, they start living together and begin to have other children; they stop receiving communion because they are now living in concubinage, and they could live so for years, attending mass every Sunday, even weekdays, without access to the Eucharist. Many years later when they have accumulated enough resources, they may then complete the traditional marriage rites before planning for the sacramental wedding.

With greater access to tertiary education however, this practice is dwindling. Access to quality and affordable education especially at tertiary level is becoming more and more a challenge, as teeming numbers of youths outdo available spaces at the public universities and the private ones are quite expensive. Without a good education, the prospect of a good job is limited; and even with a good education employment opportunities are scarce. For instance Caritas Nigeria advertised for an accounting position and got over six thousand applications! The economic crunch is a biting menace.

The Nigerian Family and Resilience:

Nevertheless the average Nigerian is known for his/her resilience, which is borne from a deep faith in God, even if that faith may not translate always to very high ethical standards. In a society so richly blessed with natural resources but so badly governed, the Church becomes a strong provider of support to the common person. Advocacy efforts are ongoing for government to recognize the cardinal principle of subsidiarity and see the Church as a partner instead. There is a lot the Church is doing in terms of access to microcredit, access to affordable quality education and health care services, which provide a veritable option to the Nigerian family, which she could do more with state funding for non-state actors like the Church. The Church should not be alternative to government though; she is only occupying a space that has been and continues to be empty. The Church in Africa therefore needs to stand by the family all the way especially in resolving issues that only the Church may resolve. For instance Episcopal Conferences need to do more to dialogue with cultures in Africa to ensure they enhance sacramental wedlock. Greater efforts at unifying the traditional with the sacramental should be made as already proposed by some episcopal conferences, therefore diminishing the economic toll on families.

Secondly Episcopal Conferences need to ensure that Catholic marriages are always protected by civil law, except where the state displays antagonism to the aims of marriage. Many priests are celebrating marriages that are not recognised by law, with the danger that often the woman is not protected when the man decides to walk away with another woman, with dire economic consequences on the woman and her children. Canon 1071(1.2) stipulates that only in a case of necessity should one assist in a marriage which 'cannot be recognized by the civil law or celebrated in accordance with it.' As a corollary Episcopal Conferences need to strengthen marriage tribunals where the marriage has become putative.[8] In some African countries there is very little professionalism with regards marriage tribunals, which are mostly constituted of priests who have other engaging pastoral obligations; there is a belief by some affected laity that because priests are not affected directly, they allow cases to linger on end, whereas the attempt often is to safeguard the bond. Some have even left the Church to Pentecostal denominations.

For us as a church, poverty is not just about family or national economy, it is about total wellbeing. Therefore as we nurture the families that are whole, we must also attempt to care in full for families that are broken. Influential Catholics, especially members of episcopal conferences should continue to leverage their relationships with those in civil authority to engage in advocacy and promote the cause of the unknown poor.

REFERENCES:

1. See Nigeria Demographics Profile, http://www.indexmundi.com/nigeria/demographics_profile.html
2. Josie Cox, Wall Street Journal Dec 19, 2014
3. The Sun Newspaper 8 December 2014, Lagos Nigeria
4. 7 June 2014 Wall Street Journal
5. Evaristus Bassey, Caritas Stylus, a Caritas Nigeria Newsletter Dec 2014
6. Personal testimony by Archbishop Ignatius Kaigama President of Nigerian Bishops Conference, December 2014
7. Elisabeth Rosenthal, New York Times 14th April 2012

The Code of Canon Law.(Theological Publications in India, Bangalore, 2005 ed), Canon 1061.

CHAPTER FIVE

THE NIGERIAN ENVIRONMENTAL REGULATORY FRAMEWORK: A CRITICAL EVALUATION

Introduction:

There is growing concern for the future of Planet Earth as a habitat for humanity, flora and fauna, mainly because of catastrophic events occasioned by climate change. In a cover story after the earthquake in Nepal, Newsweek Magazine, referring to various experts, reported that "Evidence from the end of the last Ice Age has already shown that the planet's uneasy web of seismic faults – cracks in the crust like the one that runs along the Himalayas-are very sensitive to the small pressure changes brought by change in climate. And a sensitive volcano or seismic fault-line is a very dangerous one."[1]. This goes to deepen the concern expressed in 2007 in the Intergovernmental Panel on Climate Change Synthesis Report, that, "Warming of the climate system is unequivocal, as is now evident from observations of increases in global average air and ocean temperatures, widespread melting of snow and ice, and rising global average sea level."[2]

In the most recent, Fifth Assessment Report, of IPCC it is noted that "In recent decades , changes in climate have caused impacts on natural and human systems on all continents and across the oceans. Evidence of climate –change impacts is strongest and most comprehensive for natural systems. Some impacts on human systems have also been attributed to climate change, with a major or minor contribution of climate change distinguishable from other influences…"[3]

The catastrophic impact of climate change has drawn many governments and institutions to move for conventions at global level and to domesticate policies that would create the enabling environment for the mitigation of the negative impacts . The Fifth Assessment Report has said that "Adaptation is place-and context specific, with no single approach for reducing risks appropriate across all settings. Effective risk reduction and adaptation strategies consider the dynamics of vulnerability and exposure and their linkages with socio-economic processes, sustainable development, and climate change."[3].

Being of such great concern, this seminar paper takes a look at the policy framework in Nigeria with regard to the environment. Without a regulatory framework and its enforcement, the tendency is for businesses and individuals to behave as they deem fit, sometimes falling far below the minimum standard that would make any meaningful mitigation of negative impacts. In Nigeria, the agency charged with regulating issues concerning the natural environment is National Environmental Standards and Regulations Enforcement Agency(NESREA), established by an act of parliament in 2007. In this paper the argument is that the purpose of policy is to bring change therefore little known policies and poorly implemented policies do not do justice to the raison d'etre for their formulation. The paper argues that policies that demand behavior change are better achieved if partnership with institutions or personalities that could leverage some influence is established.

 By way of approach, certain clarification of terms would be a first step; we shall then test the regulatory policies against a select focus group, and make a critique based on Laudato Si, Pope Francis' encyclical on ecology.

Clarification of Terms:

A key concept in this paper is **climate change** but before arriving at its meaning in this seminar paper, it will be necessary to look at ancillary concepts.

Weather: The Food and Agricultural Organisation, in its module on climate change and climate variability has set forward straightforward explanations of some of these concepts. Weather is described as "the day to day state of the atmosphere and its short term(from hours to a few weeks) variations such as temperature, humidity, precipitation, cloudiness, visibility or wind."[4]

Climate: On the other hand climate is defined by the Webster's College Dictionary as the 'composite or generally prevailing weather conditions of a region, as temperature, air pressure, humidity, precipitation, cloudiness, and winds, throughout the year, averaged over a series of years"[5]. Apparently therefore weather is the atmospheric condition experienced at the moment while a sustained record of that condition in a given area over several years or decades is what constitutes the climate.

Climate System: An important concept to reference is Climate system, which is explained as an "interactive system consisting of five major components: the atmosphere, the hydrosphere, the cryosphere, the land surface and the biosphere, forced or influenced by various external forcing mechanisms, the most important of which is the Sun... Also the direct effect of human activities on the climate system is considered an external forcing."[6]

FAO refers to climate variability as "the climatic parameter of a region varying from long-term mean. Every year in a particular time period, the climate of a location is different. .. These changes result from atmospheric and oceanic circulation, caused mostly by differential heating of the sun on earth."[7]

Climate Change: According to the Fifth Assessment Report, "Climate change refers to a change in the state of the climate that can be identified (e.g by using statistical tests) by changes in the in the mean and /or the variability of its properties, and that persist for an extended period , typically decades or longer."[8] The United Nations Framework Convention on Climate Change(UNFCC) makes a significant distinction. When variations occur in the climate system that is attributed to natural causes, it refers to it as climate variability, and restricts use of climate change to changes that are attributable to human activity. For the purpose of this paper, we shall go with the definition of the UNFCC found in Article 1 as follows: "a change of climate which is attributed directly or indirectly to human activity that alters the composition of the global atmosphere and which is in addition to natural climate variability observed over comparable time periods."[9]

A.Barrie Pittock a foremost authority on climate change brings additional clarification when he explains that climate change is "changes in the behavior of weather over longer time scales, such as one century to another."[10]

Our concern therefore in this paper is familiarizing ourselves with the regulatory framework the government of Nigeria has established to curtail the effect of human activity on climate. A key consequence of climate change is global warming, and as many efforts of governments all over the world are aimed at checking global warming, it would be necessary to show how these policies aim at reducing it or mitigating its impact.

Enumeration of Policies Regulating the Environment in Nigeria:

With the return to civilian rule, after about fifteen years of military rule, Nigeria decided to establish a separate ministry of environment in 1999, to pursue its efforts as signatory to the UNFCCC. The UNFCCC itself is perhaps the only incontrovertible instrument binding nations together in a united action to safeguard the climate system. There have been several attempts to come to enforceable limits of emissions, but negotiations are often politicized and leading to porous agreements. The UNFCCC " recognizes that the climate system is a shared resource whose stability can be affected by industrial and other emissions of carbon dioxide and other green house gases."[11] Nigeria as a nation prior to the return to civilian democratic rule has been part of global efforts to save the climate system. The Federal Ministry of Environment was thus established by the government of Olesegun Obasanjo to coordinate all actions of government on environmental issues and mainstream them in development plans and actions. The ministry has several parastatals among which are the National Environmental Standards Regulations Enforcement Agency(NESREA). This is the agency "empowered to enforce all environmental laws, guidelines, policies, standards and regulations in Nigeria, as well as enforcing compliance with the provisions of all international agreements, protocols, conventions and treaties on the environment to which Nigeria is a signatory."[12]

It was established in 2007.

Since its establishment NESREA has formulated some of the following regulations:

1. National Environmental (Watershed, Mountainous, Hilly and Catchment Areas) Regulations, 2009

2. National Environmental (Mining and processing of Coal, Ores and Industrial Minerals) Regulations, 2009
3. National Environmental(Chemical, Pharmaceutical, Soap and Detergent Maufacturing Industries) Regulations, 2009
4. National Environmental(Access to Genetic Resources and Benefit Sharing) Regulations 2009
5. National Environmental (Ozone Layer Protection Regulations, 2009
6. National Environmental(Textile Wearing Apparel, Leather and Footwear Industry) Regulations, 2009
7. National Environmental(Wetlands, Riverbanks and Lake Shores) Regulations, 2009
8. National Environmental(Surface and Groundwater Quality Control)Regulations,2011
9. National Environmental(Construction Sector) Regulations, 2011
10. National Environmental(Electrical/Electronic Sector) Regulations 2011
11. National Environmental(Non-metallic Minerals manufacturing Industries Sector) Regulations, 2011
12. National Environmental(Control of Vehicular Emissions from Petrol and Diesel Engines) Regulations, 2011*
13. National Environmental (Coastal and Marine Area Protection) Regulations, 2011
14. National Environmental (Protection of Endangered Species in International Trade) Regulations, 2011*
15. National Environmental (Desertification Control and Drought Mitigation) Regulation, 2011
16. National Environmeatl (Base metal, Iron and Steel Manufacturing/Recycling industries Sector) Regulations, 2011
17. National Environmental(Domestic and Industrial Plastic, Rubber and Foam Sector) Regulations 2011*

18. National Environmental(Control of Bush, Forest Fire and Open Burning) Regulations, 2011*
19. National Environmental(Quarrying and Blasting Operations) Regulations, 2013
20. National Environmental(Pulp and Paper, Wood and Wood Products Sector) Regulations, 2013

21. National Environmental(Motor Vehicle and Miscellaneous Assembly Sector) Regulations 2013
22. National Environmental(Control of Alien and Invasive Species) Regulations 2013

Detailed Description of Policy Thrusts of Selected Policies:

There are altogether over thirty regulations established by NESREA, most of which are enumerated above. However some of the policies would be selected for more detailed description based on a matrix of general-population relevance. Many of the regulations are sector specific, and though their effects affect the climate system which ultimately all, yet behavior change in that regard is limited to those in that sector. For example the regulation on the construction industry, non-metallic minerals manufacturing, base metal, iron and steel manufacturing, mining and processing of Coal, Ores and Industrial Minerals; whereas such policies as Control of Bush, Forest Fire and Open Burning, Domestic and Industrial Plastic, Rubber and Foam Sector, Protection of Endangered Species in International Trade, Control of Vehicular Emissions from Petrol and Diesel Engines, are policies which regulate behavior from a broad spectrum of the population.

1. National Environmental(Control of Bush, Forest Fire and Open Burning) Regulations, 2011:
The intendment of this regulation is to "prevent and minimize the destruction of ecosystem through fire outbreak and burning of any

material that may affect the health system through the emission of harzardous air pollutants."[13]

The regulation applies to individual persons as well as corporate entities.[14] It attempts to curtail bush burning and open fires with regard to activities such as farming, urban waste disposal, petroleum waste disposal, and the disposal of materials that produce thick and upsetting odours when burnt, such as tires, plastics. It also regulates the open burning of plant waste. Where these actions are to take place nonetheless, the agency regulates that a permit be obtained. An application to the local authorities of the agency must be made 21 days prior to the activity. The application is eventually issued by an Enforcement officer if it is found to be of merit. Indeed the regulation is so embracive that it outlaws all open burning except for barbecue grills and other outdoor cooking, camp fires, "on site burning of organic agricultural waste for subsistence farming, but not pesticides, plastics or other non-organic material." [15]. Other exceptions include for the purpose of controlling plant and animal disease[16], and the control of invasive species of plants and animals[17].

The regulation if adhered to could help reduce the effect of green house gases. In many parts of Nigeria, it is common to see open fires. These include bonfires of household junk, including high odiferous materials such as plastic, burning of tires during riots or to roast a dead animal, paper products, plant waste etc.

Until this seminar paper, I never knew that open burning of items as listed above was regulated against. I knew of course about several advisories concerning bush burning and burning of substances generally, but I did not know one needed a permit. In a survey conducted with an enlightened audience with regard to awareness concerning open burning, this was the following result:

Burning of bushes for farming purposes is common, although the law exempts those who do this for subsistence farming.

There is a great need to disseminate the regulations concerning these matters, as an adjustment in behavior will be ultimately beneficial.

2. National Environmental(Domestic and Industrial Plastic, Rubber and Foam Sector):

This policy objective is to "prevent and minimize pollution from the operations and ancillary activities of the Domestic and Industrial Plastic, Rubber and Foam Sector to the Nigerian Environment"[18]

The policy recommends the installation of relevant equipment to deal with pollution hazards as well as an emergency response plan. Industries are to ensure the detoxification of effluent material to the recommended level, as well as prevent the pollution of surface and ground water by machinery. The polluter pay principle is also adopted[19].

The policy mandates management to engage in best practices such as recycling plastics, metals, paper, wood and nylon(art7(3), and generally encourage the observation of the 5 Rs – Restore, Reduce, Recycle, Repair, Reuse, and provide protective gear to workers[20]. It goes further to direct industries to mainstream global warming prevention through use of most efficient energy technologies[21]

One of the most exciting provisions of the policy is the Extended Product Stewardship Program which has as part of its package a product Buy Back program. Schedule Xlll of the regulation mandates manufacturers and importers to see to it that a partnership is established with NESREA for this extended product stewardship program. Notwithstanding the original brand owner, industrialists and importers are 'establish a process for the collection, handling, transportation and final treatment of post-consumer products…"[22]

Citizen awareness of regulations such as this would enable them to participate in monitoring both the agency and industries. A lack of awareness would only allow room for a porous regulatory environment as the case is presently.

The regulation also restricts the release of toxic effluent and air emissions, and has established standard measures for maximum levels in the various schedules.

3. National Environmental (Control of Vehicular Emissions from Petrol and Diesel Engines) Regulations, 2011

The objective of this regulation is "to restore, preserve and improve the quality of air."[23] It is aimed at maintaining the good health especially of urban dwellers as cities are prone to pollution, by ensuring that vehicles that ply Nigerian roads have sound engine quality. It is generally accepted that fossil fuel emissions are some of the greatest causes of global warming. Global warming itself is caused by green house gases. Green house gases on their own, at the right proportion are useful for human existence. When light waves from the sun enter the atmosphere and the atmosphere becomes heated, some of the waves are radiated back into space as infrared waves. The atmosphere traps some of these outgoing waves, which help to keep our temperature at a comfortable level for human existence and other life forms. These re-radiated waves are what is called green house gases. In other planets like Venus, scientists have discovered that the green house gases are so thick that they make the planet too hot for life forms, whereas Mars barely has greenhouse gases, thereby making it too cold for various life forms. The green house gases on Earth have had such a balance ,that they have made Earth's temperatures just right for life forms. The crisis now is that the thin layer of the atmosphere is being thickened more and more by human activity, such as carbon dioxide and other green house gases emanating from fossil fuel and other industrial usages. The consequence is that much of the infrared waves that would have naturally escaped Earth's atmosphere to other parts of the universe are being trapped within the atmosphere, leading to higher temperatures on the

Earth's atmosphere and the oceans on Earth, thereby leading to warmer and warmer climate conditions.

The regulatory policy thrust therefore is to ensure that there is less harmful emissions of carbon dioxide into the atmosphere. The policy places restrictions on installation or replacement of engine units, bans two stroke engines, and vehicles without emission reduction technology.[24]. The policy provides for emission standards in Schedules 1 and lll and provides that vehicles in Nigeria shall undergo annual emission tests, except for vehicles below three years of (manufacture and) purchase.[25]

In terms of sanctions, they range from fifty thousand Naira and additional one thousand naira each day the offence continues or one year imprisonment or both for individuals, and up to five hundred thousand naira and additional twenty thousand each year the offence continues .[26]

A Critique of the Regulatory Environment

In a survey conducted with about one hundred and two persons, targeted at adequately enlightened samples of population, many of them working in Non-governmental Organizations, the result showed that 64% of the population sample did not know that all kinds of open burnings including of tires, animal and plant waste, etc required a permit; only 56% knew that vehicles with visible exhaust fumes should not be on the road and that vehicles were required to undertake emission tests, and 72% did not know about the extended buy- back program which importers and manufacturers should routinely carry out in order to make better use of post- consumer products.

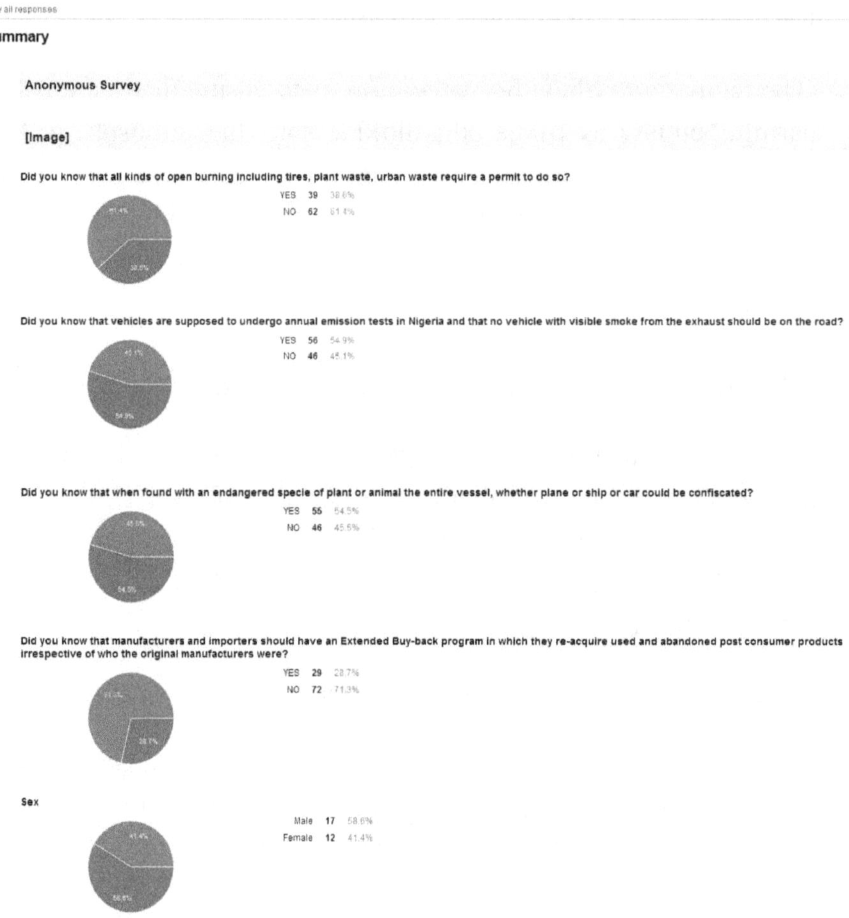

With this result which is from an enlightened audience, one can imagine the level of awareness existing among barely literate and unexposed citizens in a country where the adult literacy rate is 51.1%, according to UNICEF[27]. One could conclude safely that majority of citizens are ignorant of many of the regulations. Where there is awareness of regulations, the enforcement is weak. The consequence would be that factors that cause global warming such as industrialization, the energy system for both industrial and domestic use, the transport system, poor agricultural practices, deforestation, poor waste management and so on, will persist, with ultimate negative impact on sustainable development. Sustainable development has as one of its pillars concern for the natural environment.

It does appear that Nigeria establishes these regulations in order to align with the international best practices, but the enforcement is weak because of weak institutions. Often the institutions are poorly funded, or the funding is misapplied or simply embezzled. Poor institutions are a reflection of a weak or failing state. Fukayama said of Nigeria: "Nigeria's real institutional deficit lies in the…: lack of strong modern and capable state and absence of rule of law that provides property rights, citizens security, and transparency in transactions. These two deficits are related. Rather than having a modern state that can provide necessary public goods like roads, ports, schools, and public health on an impersonal basis, the Nigerian government main activities is predatory or…prebendal: it is engaged in extraction of rent and their distribution to other members of political elites. This leads to the routine violation of the rule of law…"[28] (Fukuyama, 2014).

The pathway to an effective regulatory environment is citizen buy in. Ownership comes through awareness and education and interest. Government alone cannot do this. It may not have the capacity to present matters from the self-interest (not selfish-interest) of the citizenry, especially where trust has gone down. An effective regulatory environment may therefore require partnerships between government and non- state actors.

Recently Pope Francis published an encyclical letter called *Laudato Si*, in which the main thrust was integral ecology. "When we fail to acknowledge as part of reality the worth of a poor person, a human embryo, a person with disabilities…it becomes difficult to hear the cry of nature itself; everything is connected."[29](Francis, 2015, 117).

The idea is that underlying the factors enumerated above that cause global warming, the attitude of the human person to the natural order is a significant factor. In *Laudato Si*, Pope Francis pushes hard for a change of attitude. This advocacy is likely to do a lot more than the regulatory policies on their own may have done. Partnership with civil society organizations is therefore crucial for success of policies that require popular adherence.

REFERENCES

[1]BENTON, A . (2015) Nepal Earthquake Could Have Been a Manmade Disaster As Climate Change Brings Seismic Shift. *Newsweek Magazine*. 08.05.2015 no 19 pp 14-19

[2] INTERGOVERNMENTAL PANEL ON CLIMATE CHANGE. *Climate Change 2007: Synthesis Report*. Valencia: IPCC Plenary XXVll.　　p.(30)　　[Online].　　Accessed　　from www.ipcc.ch/.../assessment-report/... [Accessed on July 6th 2015].

[3]. IPCC,2014: Summary for Policymakers. In :*Climate Change 2014: Impacts, Adaptation and Vulnerability .Part A: Global and Sectoral Aspects. Contribution of Working Group ll to the Fifth Assessment Report of the Intergovernmental Panel on Climate Change.* Field, C.B.et al (eds). Cambridge and New York: Cambridge University Press. p.5

[4]FAO Module 1 Understanding Climate Variability and Climate Change.　　[Online]　　Accessed　　from ftp://ftp.fao.org/docrep/.../a1247e02.pdf   [Accessed on July 6th 2015]

[5]*Random House Kernerman Webster's College Dictionary*. (2010) . London: Random House, Inc.

[6] BAEDE, A.P.M. et al. Climate System: An Overview. [Online] Accessed from www.grida.no/climate/ipcc.../tar-01.pdf [Accessed on July 6th 2015]

[7] FAO Module 1 Understanding Climate Variability and Climate Change. [Online] Accessed from ftp://ftp.fao.org/docrep/.../a1247e02.pdf [Accessed on July 6th 2015]

[8] IPCC,2014 p.5

[9] UNFCC Article 1.[Online] Accessed from www.unfcc.int. [Accessed on 6th July 2015].

[10]PITTOCK, B. (2009) *Climate Change:The Science, Impacts and Solutions.* ,Melbourne: CSIRO Publishers. P.(3).

[11]unfccc.int

[12] Federal Ministry of Environment. [Online] . Accessed from http://www.climatechange.gov.ng/index.php/fme/special-fme-units. [Accessed on 7th July 2015].

[13] NIGERIA.FEDERAL MINISTRY OF ENVIRONMENT. *National Environmental(Control of Bush, Forest Fire and Open Burning) Regulations, 2011.* Part 1, no.1 S.I. No.15 of 2011.

[14]Ibid no.2

[15]Ibid no.22c

[16]Ibid no.22e

[17]Ibid no.22f

[18] NIGERIA. FEDERAL MINISTRY OF ENVIRONMENT. *National Environmental(Domestic and Industrial Plastic, Rubber and Foam Sector* S.I. No.17 of 2011. Art.2

[19] Ibid. Art.5,6

[20] Ibid. Art7(6)

[21] Ibid. Art 8

[22] Ibid Schedule Xllla

[23] NIGERIA. FEERAL MINISTRY OF ENVIRONMENT. *National Environmental (Control of Vehicular Emissions from Petrol and Diesel Engines) Regulations, 2011.* Art.1

[24] Ibid Art. 3

[25] Ibid Art.9(2b and c)

[26] Ibid Art. 30(1 and 2)

[27] www.unicef.org/…/Nigeria_statistics.html

[28] FUKAYAMA, F. (2014) *Political Order and Political Decay.* London: Profile Books. P. 238

[29] Francis, P.(2015) *Laudato Si.* Vatican: Vatican Publications . no.117

CHAPTER SIX

ORGANISING FOR GOOD GOVERNANCE[*]
A KEY NOTE ADDRESS PRESENTED AT A STRATEGIC THINKING WORKSHOP ORGANISED BY MISEREOR ON HUMAN RIGHTS AND GOVERNANCE IN NIGERIA

I thank the Dialogue and Partnership director of Misereor in Nigeria, Mr. Cosmas Olaniyan for extending this invitation to me in my capacity as Director Church and Society, Catholic Secretariat of Nigeria. Misereor has invested a lot of resources in Nigeria. I was always afraid that there was too much presupposition of capacity by Misereor of the partners, as in the past, Misereor had not done very much in terms of partner trainings and accompaniment. With the dialogue and partnership office however a lot is being done in terms of accompaniment; there are regular visits by the partnership director, which I believe accompany the local partners appropriately in developing their systems and processes therefore enhancing effectiveness in outputs and results, and starting from the immediate past director, there have been several learning and capacity building sessions for partners.

This workshop at this time is quite timely. The government is still new in all sense of the word, especially being that after about four months, ministers are yet to assume duties at the federal level. Some state governors too are only just appointing commissioners. Some local governments are either rounding off their tenure or assuming fresh tenures. The workshop provides an opportunity therefore to tie in with the agenda of government at all levels and ensure the participation of the people and promote the common good.

The scope of the workshop is impressive, as it does injury to the mindset of the average Nigerian. The average Nigerian thinks of government as the federal government. The pothole on the road that passes by his/her compound is seen as the responsibility of the federal government; the poor health infrastructure, the inadequate water resources, in deed all gaps in governance are blamed on the federal government. Perhaps this is deserving, because even as we claim to be a federation, we operate sometimes as a unitary government, with the powers of our central government so strong, because it is a revenue sharer to all tiers; and since the early seventies a dependency culture has been nurtured, in which many states on their own are not sustainable but have to depend on the monthly allocation that comes from the federation account. On the part of the states and citizenry this dependency bred a lax culture of taxation, in which citizens did not feel the pinch of being taxed for governance and so had no real stake in ensuring accountability. State emperors or governors as they are called, were quite happy to be left alone to (mis)appropriate the funds as they chose, since they didn't come from the people directly. With the present economic downturn and the diminishing returns from the federation account, many state governments would be forced to be innovative; and the recent quest to beef up internally generated revenue may have forced many governments to apply all forms of taxation on the citizens, and hopefully because of the inconvenience, there would be a sustained backlash of genuinely demanding accountability, so that when we say "tax payers' money", it would really be the money you wouldn't want to see wasted, because of the pain of parting with it, which you could have used to solve your needs but which you are being compelled to give to government as tax. The three areas of this workshop, namely governance, human rights and justice and community development in my mind, factor in a scope that involves the engagement of government at all relevant levels especially the local government level. Just a few days ago, we called on the National Assembly to revisit the issue of local government autonomy, with the argument that if the corrupt laws enacted by state assemblies to amass local government revenues were abrogated and local governments had access to their funding, then the local people would be more keen in monitoring for accountability.

The Opportunity of the SDGs

Permit me to say that perhaps the most momentous opportunity for this workshop is the recent launch of the Sustainable Development Agenda. As you know the MDGs were given a terminal date of 2015, from 2000 when they were adopted. The SDGs also have a life span of 15 years but with a more ambitious agenda of 17 goals and 169 targets. The SDGs were adopted at the UN General Assembly in September 2015, with some of us being present, having also contributed in some small measure through civil society groups and working groups of international Catholic organizations. I mention the SDGs because, if we tie in our interventions and initiatives to the framework, we would not only be changing our communities but achieving a global agenda. The SDGs represent yet the boldest step by the world as a whole to transform our world and impact on five critical areas : People, Planet, Prosperity, Peace and Partnership. The Heads of State make bold to say:

> " *We resolve, between now and 2030, to end poverty and hunger everywhere; to combat inequalities within and among countries; to build peaceful, just and inclusive societies; to protect human rights and promote gender equality; and to ensure the lasting protection of the planet and its natural resources....*

As we embark on this great collective journey, we pledge that no one will be left behind. Recognizing that the dignity of the human person is fundamental, we wish to see the Goals and targets met for all nations and peoples and for all economic and social groupings. And we will endeavour to reach the furthest behind first."(Transforming Our World: The 2030 Agenda for Sustainable Development, p.3)

Let me also quote a relevant section of the vision of this great agenda:

"We envisage a world of universal respect for human rights and human dignity, the rule of law, justice, equality and non-discrimination; of respect for race, ethnicity and cultural diversity; and of equal opportunity permitting the full realization of human potential and contributing to shared prosperity. A world which invests in its children and in which every child grows up free from violence and exploitation. A world in which every woman and girl enjoys full gender equality and all legal, social and economic barriers to their empowerment have been removed. A just, equitable, tolerant, open and socially inclusive world in which the needs of the most vulnerable are met."(ibid,p.4)

We as agents of the church are not an alternate government, the church is never an alternative government. It is just that in a society where those in public service have not fully understood the task of good governance and end up serving themselves, the result is the poverty we see around, and the church, desperate to attend to the needs of people begins to implement services which would normally have been reserved for government. Sometimes government gets so lazy and comfortable that they relax and let the church carry the burden. So our task would be to engage our governments at all levels first of all to understand these resolves and this vision of the SDGs, and further engage them to embark on the kind of good governance that would contribute towards the attainment of the overall vision.

The Right to Good Governance

A rights based approach to development presupposes an understanding of fundamental rights and other rights, and overriding the patronage mentality of government officials whom we celebrate whereas they were doing what they ought to do; it is a firm belief in distributive justice and ensuring that everyone, every community, deserves to live in dignity, not because they have an indigene from their area or an in-law or a friend. In Nigeria, this is our main problem. According to Fukayama (2014 p.(225)) in his latest book entitled ***Political Order and Political Decay,*** "The Nigerian State is weak not only in technical capacity and its ability to enforce laws impersonally and transparently. It is also weak in a moral sense. It has a deficit of legitimacy. There is little loyalty to a nation called Nigeria that supersedes ties to one's region, ethnic group, or religious community." What you would have in this kind of space is that very little is done out of a sense of justice or the common good.

I was listening to a lecture one day, and the lecturer was saying that there are no inalienable rights. That if there was such a thing, how come it took the world so long to declare them? How come that even after such a historical declaration in 1948 on December 10th people have to still struggle for their rights? His conclusion was that in all circumstances, human rights have to be fought for, they have to be struggled for; they are not just given. This might be an extreme position, for come to think of it, ever since the declaration of fundamental rights, a lot of progress has been achieved. Many constitutions of the world now enshrine these rights, and the good thing is that when they are infringed upon, there is a means of redress, through the courts. In Nigeria there is even a Human Rights

Commission. Just last week I heard over Channels TV that a group had come into Nigeria from the UN to review the laws that were preventing a proper enjoyment of human rights by Nigerians, if I understood them well.

Nevertheless, while many nations of Europe take these rights for granted, the average person in Nigeria and several African nations still undergoes abuse by the Big man. The police is being used to arrest and detain people for civil offences; rich people can manipulate magistrates to imprison the person that crosses their path, and worse of all, many communities have no access to water, good roads, good schools and health facilities and live without dignity. There are millions of people who are living below the poverty level. It is said that after China and India, Nigeria has the greatest number of poor persons comparatively. This means that in a population of about 178 million persons, even if you say that the poverty ratio is now 33.6%, about 54 million Nigerians are living in extreme deprivation, which is the population of several of our West African nations put together. This is not right in a country that is not poor at all, a country that has earned billions of dollars from oil in the last forty years.

To conceptualize what we mean by deprivation let me refer to an authority.

According to D. Gordon(2005), "deprivation can be conceptualized as a continuum which ranges from no deprivation through mild, moderate and severe deprivation to extreme deprivation." He went on to list conditions which when two or more are absent, would indicate an absolute poverty threshold. Below are the 7 poverty indicators for those in the range of youths:

1. **Food** – there is absolute poverty if the body mass index is 18.5 or below, showing severe food deprivation (underweight)
2. **Water** - when available sources are limited to open sources such as wells, springs or surface water and it takes longer than a 30 minute round trip to access

3. **Sanitation** – when there is no access to toilet facilities of any kind or those available are unimproved facilities such as pour flush latrines; covered pit latrines; and buckets
4. **Health** – when a woman has no access to treatment for a serious ailment or a pregnant woman cannot receive antenatal care from a trained personnel who knows the modes of transmission and prevention of HIV/AIDS; or when a man does not receive treatment over a serious ailment or does not know the mode of transmission and prevention of HIV/AIDS.
5. **Shelter** – when more than three persons have to live in a room, where the building has no flooring and is made of mud, and where the roof is made mostly of natural materials like thatch.
6. **Education** – where the person did not complete basic education and or is illiterate
7. **Information** – where there is no access to mass broadcast media at home eg radio and television. (See GORDON, D.(2005) Indicators of Poverty and Hunger. *Expert Group Meeting on Youth development Indicators. United Nations Headquarters New York December 12th – 14th December 2005 .p.3)*

Of course with the advancement in our world, under information, we would have to include not having a mobile phone and access to internet as a possible condition of living in extreme deprivation.

The above analysis means that these seven areas are so basic that when two or more of them are absent at any given time, the deprivation is extreme and the person fails to live in dignity, which means the person is not enjoying his life and right to dignity as a human being.

We cannot keep silent in the face of these inequalities and injustices. There are no supermen and superwomen while the rest are inferior beings. We are compelled by our social teaching to promote the dignity of those in our communities by engaging with government at all levels to ensure there is a minimum of development for all, for development is the opposite of poverty.

Catholic Social Teaching

Catholic Social Thought provides a basis for development as a right. Every human being, because each one is made in the image and likeness of God is seen as full of dignity irrespective of class or political affiliation.

The human being is like no other creature on earth. S/he alone so far is known to have self-awareness or self-consciousness, and by " his power to know himself in the depths of his being he rises above the whole universe of mere objects." S/he has an intellect with a capacity to know both empirical truth and higher truths. S/he is also endowed with a conscience, a self- regulating law that is written in his/her heart. "His conscience is man's most secret core, and his sanctuary." (See Gaudium et Spes no. 16). Above all s/he has the gift of freedom which allows him/her make free choices rather than driven by mere instinct or compelled by external forces. Man is not created to be alone, they are made male and female by God.

Dignity guarantees human rights. Each human being deserves the best of treatment, access, facilities, respect, because s/he has this inherent dignity.

In contrast to an atheistic anthropology which puts man above all things and puts none above him/her, as if doing so depletes man's dignity, "the church holds that to acknowledge God is in no way to oppose the dignity of man, since such dignity is grounded and brought to perfection in God." (See Gaudium et Spes no. 21)

Christianity believes in the superiority of the human being over all created things but that it is God that puts these things under man's charge, which s/he uses to his/her joy and satisfaction, to the glory of God.

The fullness of this dignity is realized in Jesus Christ, by the very fact that he assumed human nature, suffered, died, rose from death, and raised that nature to a 'dignity beyond compare'.

Every development effort should therefore consciously reflect the fact that people are not mere statistics but persons dignified by God in Christ. John Paul ll said in Centesimus Annus, "We are not dealing with people in the 'abstract,' but with real, 'concrete', 'historical' people. We are dealing with *each individual*, since each one is included in the mystery of the Redemption, and through this mystery Christ has united himself with each one forever." (no. 53). In his address at the UN recently, Pope Francis appealed to world leaders to realise that the decisions or inactions they make impact on real living persons who suffer under the yoke of such decisions or inactions.

An elevated understanding of the human being as one inherently dignified and by God, should lead to accelerated action on those who are deprived, to whom we have a preferential option to work for and defend.

It means it is our responsibility to continue to communicate this consciousness of dignity to those in charge of affairs, to appeal to their consciences, to monitor the abuse of this dignity, to engage with all stakeholders for the upholding of this dignity. In the opening of Populorum Progressio, Pope Paul Vl said *"the development of peoples has the Church's close attention, particularly the development of those peoples who are striving to escape from hunger, misery, endemic disease and ignorance; of those who are looking for a wider share in the benefits of civilization and a more active improvement of their human qualities; of those who are aiming purposefully at their complete fulfillment.*" (no.1) We cannot let ourselves or our church down.

Paths We Can Take

Let me suggest some ways in which we could carry out this conversation and engagement:

1. Metanoia:

To embark on a rights based approach to development means we believe that every person deserves access to resources not as a favour but as his/her due. This would mean believing firmly in solidarity, believing strongly in eliminating inequalities. Goal 10 of the SDGs talks about reducing inequalities. We cannot embark on a task of removing inequalities if we do not firmly believe in solidarity and convince others to. Therefore we embrace Pope Francis' call for a conscious decision to engage in a mental turn around that sees solidarity as restoring to the poor what belongs to them. We must believe in the 'universal destination' of the goods of the earth, as the Stewardship principle tells us. We must firmly believe in the common good. Without this mental conversion, according to Pope Francis, even if structures are put in place, they eventually become "corrupt, oppressive and ineffectual."(Se Evangelii Gaudi no.189). Earlier on Pope St. John Paul had said that "Solidarity is not a feeling of vague compassion or shallow distress at the misfortunes of so many people, both near and far. On the contrary, it is a firm and persevering determination to commit oneself to the common good; that is to say, to the good of all and of each individual, because we are all really responsible for all."(See Solicitudo rei Socialis no.38). If we don't have this theological framework, we will just be like any other civil servant who is just making the routines of work.

2. Develop Strategies:

We then have to develop strategies, which is what this workshop is about. Setting up community based development units that feed into an overarching diocesan coordination mechanism and ultimately into a national coordination role is an essential strategy. We already have the diocesan JDPCs, what of the parish or community based ? The danger is that when these structures are set, they are left on their own without adequate support, monitoring and evaluation. Part of strategy will be to develop multi-year strategic plans which are broken down into annual work plans. Even at parish or grassroots level, this must be done.

These plans can be based on the Sustainable Development Goals Framework and fit into the overall pastoral plan of the dioceses and perhaps the national, to avoid a situation where the interventions are seen as a stand- alone, differently from the integrated mission of the church.

Massive awareness creation will have to be made concerning the 2030 agenda itself as the framework agenda of the church in its outreach to society. Church gate keepers such as Bishops, Parish priests, Parish Sisters, Catechists are very important targets because they occupy leadership positions and could transmit this to their congregations. They should thus be engaged. A very important element of this animation is to reiterate the three-fold dimension of mission of the church, with sustainable charity as an essential element. Bishops and Priests would do far better if they realize and believed that charity is beyond the personal level and must be organized as an essential activity of the church according to the Motu Proprio of Benedict XVl on Charity. Just to remind you, the Pope repeated what he said in Deus Caritas Est that *"The Church's deepest nature* is expressed in her three-fold responsibility: of proclaiming the word of God (*kerygma-martyria*), celebrating the sacraments (*leitourgia*) and exercising the ministry of charity (*diakonia*). These duties presuppose each other and are inseparable" (*Deus Caritas Est*, 25). So he said that charity must be organised at all levels if it is to be sustainable. 'The Church is... called as a whole to the exercise of the *diakonia* of charity, whether in the small communities of particular Churches or on the level of the universal Church. This requires organization "if it is to be an ordered service to the community" (cf. *ibid.*, 20), an organization which entails a variety of institutional expressions.' (Motu Proprio).

3. **Campaign for Justiciability**:

We could start a campaign for the justiciability of the socio-economic rights. When something is justiciable it means we can go to court and claim it if we are deprived. The fundamental rights are justiciable but the socio-economic rights are not. But I think we can use the framework of the Sustainable Development Goals to pursue an agenda for justiciability of the socio-economic rights especially in the context of a government that claims to be progressive. Recently there was talk of bringing back the unsigned copy of the amendment of the constitution to the President for his assent; in that amendment there was a provision which would have made basic education and basic health a right. We could work with our representatives to extend these to include shelter and the right to food, so that social protection measures would be taken by government at all levels as a matter of justice.

Even if our target to amend the constitution is not achieved, at state and local government level, let us open up as a matter of policy, to engage the legislative arms of our various governments. Staying aside and complaining should no longer be the case. Do our councilors know us ? Do our Assembly Reps know us ? Can they listen to us ? Do our National Assembly Representatives know us ? Can we learn to study the laws and policies of our states that affect the areas of our interventions and do our best to consult experts who could help us with relevant policy briefs?

4. Try Influencing the Budget:

Have we done a needs assessments of communities you work in? Have we engaged them for them to come to consciousness of their situation, and have you sensitized them to know that they could do something about it? Can you work with them to input their needs in the budget? Have you researched on the budget process in your local government, and if there is no process in your LGA, who can you engage to institute a process? Are you part of a **coalition** in the state that can engage with government on the budget process so that the inputs serve reflect critical areas rather than profligacy? Remember that most often budgets are tailored to the needs of government ministries and parastatals. Does your coalition have enough leverage to engage with any relevant ministries ?

5. Do not Wait for Elections…Engage Structures:

Let us not wait for elections before we engage with our communities. Let us interact with them and educate them about political engagement; let us work with them to raise score cards of those who serve them, and use that to engage political office holders through town hall meetings. Let us form a habit of writing to government institutions and visiting them to engage them on their missions. Goal 16 of the SDGs says : *Promote peaceful and inclusive societies for sustainable development, provide access to justice for all and build effective, accountable and inclusive institutions at all levels.* This is why a workshop such as this is very important because we should be able to come out with sustainable ways of engaging with the institutions that affect our lives: Public Complaints, Code of Conduct, the Judiciary, the legislature, EFCC, ICPC, the Police, the private sector etc. There is protection of rights only when strong institutions enhance the rule of law. Where individuals are more powerful than institutions, there can be no rule of law. We have a moral duty, in our own little ways, to ensure that we help to keep our institutions strong.

6. And Where We can Provide Service…

And where we can provide service, let us do so with all professionalism and ethics. If we criticize government we must endeavor to rise above the standards which we criticize. We have to be humble enough to sit down and learn what we do not know and be sincere enough to put it into practice. We have to resist the infection of corruption which is like a pandemic in our country Nigeria.

CONCLUSION: Beyond Rhetorics

We have to engage as a matter of policy and action. We have to reach out and influence. We have secluded ourselves for too long and done our own thing for too long. We have to cultivate our own constituency first by engaging our own people and building a critical mass of support; at the same time we could reach out to high net worth individuals who could be our allies, and other organisations who could partner with us. Goal 17 talks of means of implementation, which has a lot to do with partnerships. Let us realise that to work for the poor, to engage on their behalf, we need to build a formidable base. Thank you.

CHAPTER SEVEN

ENGAGING FOR COMPARABLE EXCELLENCE: A STUDY OF STAFF ATTRITION AMONG FAITH-BASED HEALTH FACILITIES IN NIGERIA

1.0 INTRODUCTION

Catholic Health facilities account for the largest number of faith based treatment facilities in Nigeria. The Catholic Church as a member of the Christian Health Association of Nigeria(CHAN) has approximately 1367 facilities ranging mostly between primary health centres(PHC) and secondary facilities. Ownership of these facilities is between Dioceses and Religious Congregations. Even when parishes establish and run primary or secondary health facilities, the legal ownership resides within the Diocese. The management of many of the Diocesan health facilities is entrusted to Religious Congregations with relevant charisms, with some managed directly by designated diocesan officials . Many of the human resources for health(HRH) decisions in terms of hiring, promotion, transfers are carried out by the management boards of these institutions with strong input from the Administrators.

In 2010 the Catholic Bishops' Conference of Nigeria established Catholic Caritas Foundation of Nigeria(CCFN, also known as Caritas Nigeria) as a development and humanitarian organization coordinating the efforts of the church in this sector. This role is being performed in collaboration with relevant units of Church and Society Department of the Catholic Secretariat of Nigeria depending on the development or humanitarian issue at hand. In order to achieve professionalism, Caritas Nigeria was registered with Corporate Affairs Commission . Caritas Nigeria has since its establishment undertaken site management as a sub-recipient of the AIDSRelief grant from Catholic Relief Services(CRS), and from Christian Health Association of Nigeria. In 2012 Caritas Nigeria won a five year grant from the Centre for Disease Control and Prevention(CDC) for comprehensive HIV/AIDS intervention in faith based facilities called Sustainable HIV/AIDS Intervention Action in Nigeria(SUSTAIN). As a result of that intervention, Caritas Nigeria is currently supporting 30 Comprehensive Care & Treatment (CCT) facilities, 99 PMTCT facilities and 7 CBOs which are supporting services for community HIV Testing & Counselling (HTC), Orphans & Vulnerable Children (OVC) and HIV Prevention Activities. This represents an expansion from SUSTAIN Year I levels to include 7 newly activated Comprehensive Care and Treatment facilities (CCTs), 12 newly activated Prevention of Mother To Child Transmission sites as well as 3 new Community Based Organisations to do Community HIV Testing and Counseling (HTC).

Thus in its second year, the SUSTAIN Project is providing 101,504 adults and children living with HIV with a minimum of one care service, out of which 50,205 adults and children are receiving lifesaving Antiretroviral Therapy across twelve states: Benue, Kogi, Nassarawa, Plateau, Kaduna, Delta, Ondo, Ogun, Ekiti, Osun and Oyo and the Federal Capital Territory, Abuja.

In the course of the intervention Caritas Nigeria has encountered site specific challenges and issues that run across. One of the prevalent challenges is that of staff attrition.

In the month of June 2014, the Executive Secretary of Caritas Nigeria attended a Human Resources for Health program in the Harvard School of Public Health. Though the focus of the program was mainly on public health institutions in terms of strategizing for HRH composition and distribution for better health care delivery, Fr. Evaristus Bassey decided to make a study of the recurring issue of staff attrition in faith based health facilities in order to advise the leadership of the Church which constitutes most of the ownership. At the presentation of the Executive Secretary's report to the Caritas Nigeria Board, this issue was noted by the chairman of the Board, and Fr. Evaristus Bassey the Executive Secretary informed the board that he had planned already to make a study of the issue as a direct output of his course in Harvard School of Public Health. The work would not have been possible however without the significant contribution of Caritas Nigeria staff who assisted with the questionnaire and were sent to the field. The hope is that this report would contribute to addressing the issue, leading to greater health outcomes.

2.0 CONTEXT

The analysis of context is done looking at the political, economic, social, technological, environmental and legal (PESTEL) situation existing in the operational environment. Country wide information is not given here as this is intended to be a study with a focused audience. Suffice it to say that in Nigeria the Federal Government generally makes policies that regulate health care without precluding the role of State governments in formulating their own policies or adapting federal policies to suit their environment. Local governments also establish and run health care facilities at community level. The Federal government established the National Primary Health Care Development Agency(NPHCDA) which attempts to coordinate the sector especially HRH issues at that level. Some states are also establishing State primary Health Care Development Agencies, e.g Nasarawa State. Faith based facilities mostly are at PHC level, with some secondary level facilities. Though they are independent, usually they have to meet standards set by governments at all levels.

Faith based institutions operate in an 'indifferent' **political** environment. In 2015, an opposition government for the first time in Nigeria won elections against an incumbent administration.

President Muhammadu Buhari thus rules over Nigeria as President and Commander in Chief of the Armed Forces. Other arms of government are a bi-cameral National Assembly and the Judiciary. Of the 36 executive governors in charge of the States, and the 36 unicameral houses of assembly, not more than three states have established any meaningful partnerships with the church for social services. Apart from Anambra, Ebonyi, Benue, there is no information showing collaboration between state governments and church authorities resulting in financial support to health facilities run by the church. Anambra State not only collaborates in health systems strengthening with the church but also supports the schools owned and run by the church, which were handed over to their original owners. Anambra does this under a legal instrument established through an executive bill. Cross River State government has supported mission schools like St. Patrick's College, Ikot Ansa and Hope Waddel College; however these have been in terms of grants for renovations. Akwa Ibom State government under Governor Emmanuel Udom has supported the renovation of St. Luke's Hospital Anua, one of the oldest health facilities in the country but there is yet no legal instrument for such collaboration. There is no information too that any of the 774 Local Government Areas(LGAs), supports the efforts of faith based organizations(FBOs) in the area of primary health care.

The **economic** context in which FBOs operate in Nigeria is one in which they have to compete with facilities of government whose salary of staff is part of government budget. Although in the first and second quarters of 2016 the Nigerian economy practically went into a recession, this practice is sure to remain, especially as the Buhari government began full implementation of the single treasure account (TSA) policy in which all revenue made by parastatals and agencies of government are lodged in a single government account. The withdrawal of federal government funds from the banking sector has shrunk the financial and profit base of many of the institutions, leading to massive retrenchment in the sector. The low earning into the federal account due to dwindling oil prices has led many states into economic challenges, manifesting especially in a backlog of unpaid salaries. Many states are resorting to a second bailout from the federal government. The down turn in the economy has led to double digit inflation of up to 16 %. Added with the adoption of the flexible exchange rate policy, an analysis of the poverty ratio would probably show that millions of Nigerians have descended below the poverty rate. FBO facilities pay their staff from user fees and thus have a challenge balancing both operational and allocative efficiency of resources. The challenge most of them have is that no matter how low the user fees are, there are many defaulters who cause the facilities to be in perennial financial straits because of the economic condition of the end users.

The existence of private sector is a major threat to the human resources for health of FBOs. Members of the private sector collect high user fees which attract an exclusive clientele among high income earners and are therefore able to invest in highly qualified specialists. Some of the private facilities are owned by specialists who also work full time in government tertiary health facilities. Foreign Partner Agencies have over time provided limited leverage for faith based facilities in terms of access to test kits, selected medication and equipment but this is not enough and therefore unsustainable.

Socially, there is a mentality that health institutions run by the church should be free of user-fees or at the most unsustainably lowest rate. This mentality is enhanced by the high poverty rate and the number of unemployed. FBOs have a post-economic motivation which mainly has to do with the salvation of the human being with Man/Woman being seen as a child of God with inherent dignity; there is thus an almost rights based approach to health care supply which underlies the reason those without fee capacity are not turned away or aggressively dealt with.

Technologically, many FBOs that have support from foreign partner agencies have basic diagnostic equipment especially in the area of HIV diagnosis and treatment. The bigger FBO facilities may also be competing with government and private sector in the acquisition of high tech diagnostic equipment but this is limited. Opportunities exist to apply mobile Health(mHealth) or eHealth especially as many FBO facilities are located in hard to reach areas, and as many of Nigeria's facilities still lag behind in the application of technology. Protocols developed could be used in rural health provision. Health outreaches are great opportunities to drive demand for services. Nigeria's teledensity of over 140 million (NCC March 2016) is a great opportunity.

FBOs have strong stewardship towards the **environment**. The low awareness of the general population on environmental issues is an opportunity for FBOs to promote the linkage between environment and health. The Fifth Assessment Report by the IPCC (www.ipcc.ch) is a useful information tool as well as the impetus given by Pope Francis on Laudato Si and the COP 21 agreements in Paris in December of 2015.

The National Health Bill was translated into an Act when it was signed into law by President Goodluck Jonathan weeks before he left office in 2015. It has become the main framework law to guide the health sector in Nigeria. Even in this Act, there is no distinctive recognition of Faith Based facilities, rather they are lumped under private, and the act makes no specific provision for Faith Based Facilities(FBF) in the funding grid, even as it makes an attempt to project basic health care as a right. The Legal framework in most parts of Nigeria generally therefore has not made room for the accommodation of non-state bodies in state budgets even in a matter as important as health; the budget is still seen as a state exclusive instrument. This offers opportunities for FBOs to advocate for change. Lobby has already started on this, but there will be need to benchmark with neighbouring countries' data or global data to see what countries in the sub region or around the world establish such partnerships . Successful advocacy would see state allocations going for service delivery in faith based health facilities(FBF). Hopefully government would realize that they are only stewards of resources that belong to all, especially in a context where natural resources account for most of the GDP. However great opportunities exist with the National Health Act and these opportunities should be explored and exploited.

3.0 OBJECTIVES OF STUDY

This study has the following objectives:

1. Trace the fundamental cause(s) of staff attrition in Faith Based(Catholic) Facilities
2. Make recommendations in order to influence change through entrenchment of standard HRH practices

3.1 Scope

The survey was targeted at faith-based facilities within the Nigerian health and development sector covering the six geopolitical regions of the country to ensure nationwide coverage; however because of threat of Boko Haram the North East region was excluded from the study. 13 health facilities altogether were visited.

3.2 Approach and Methodology

The approach adopted was survey and questionnaire distribution to the target group. Oral interviews were also conducted through telephone.

Three sets of questionnaires were designed for the following set of respondents in each of the selected facilities namely:

- Hospital Administrators
- Current workers (staff still working in the hospital)
- Past workers and (those who had left the facility in question)

The questionnaires were administered within the same period in each of the thirteen sites.

The ones for past workers were administered remotely through telephone interview.

All administered questionnaires were collected and the responses collated and analyzed using Epi Info, the CDC/WHO Health Survey software.

These facilities include:

   i. St Anne's Hospital Molete
  ii. Our Lady's Hospital Iseyin
 iii. Annunciation Hospital Emene
  iv. St Joseph's Hospital Adazi-Nnukwu
   v. Our Lady of Waters Bomadi
  vi. Assumption Catholic Hospital Warri
 vii. Bishop Murray Medical Centre, Makurdi
viii. St Charles Hospital Adoka
  ix. St Gerard's Hospital Kaduna

   x. St Louis Hospital Zonkwa

   xi. St Francis Hospital Jambutu

  xii. Shuwa Maternity

 xiii. Sisters of Nativity Hospital, Jikwoyi, Abuja

4.0 COMPARATIVE AND DESRIPTIVE ANALYSISs

Total number of Facilities surveyed = 13

Total number of Respondents = 107

      — Hospital Administrators = 13

      — Current workers = 63

      — Past workers = 33

4.1 HOSPITAL ADMINISTRATORS' CATEGORY

4.1.1 Age/Gender Distribution

Among this category interviewed, 46 % were above 51 years old, 23% were in the age bracket between 41 and 50, while 23% were between 31 to 40 years old.

Of this lot, 69% are females. This is because most of the facilities are headed by female Religious.

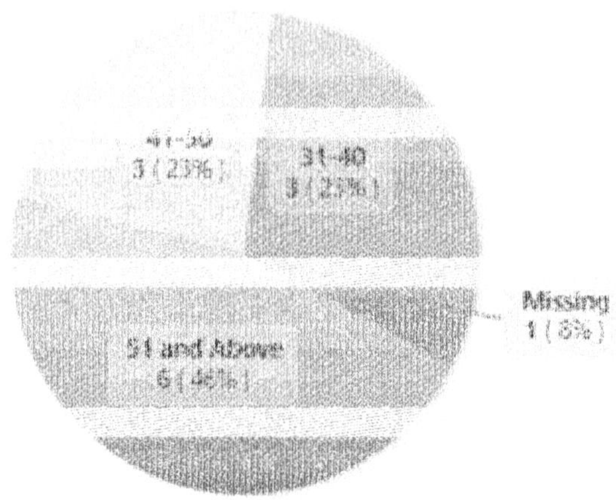

Age Distribution

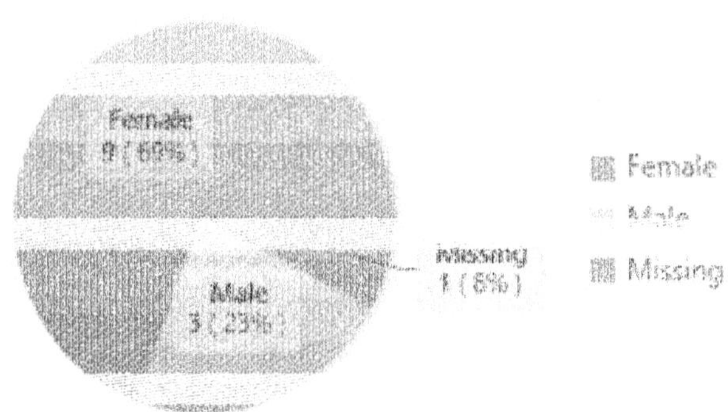

Gender Distribution

4.1.2 Number of Years of Work in the Facility:

While 33% have worked for about a year in a particular hospital, 25% have worked for a maximum of three years while 41% have worked between 3 to 5 years.

How long have you been employed by this Hospital?	Frequency	Percent
0	4	33.33 %
1	3	25.00 %
3	5	41.67 %
TOTAL	12	100.00 %

Duration staff worked in the hospital

As administrators, majority of them(41%) have been in the position for about a year, while 25% have occupied the position between 3 and five years.

Duration in office as administrator

4.1.3 Human Resources Unit:

When asked about a human resources unit or point person, 54% of the Administrators admitted to not having one. 8% admitted to not knowing while 38% responded in the affirmative. The matter got worse when asked about the existence of a human resources policy; only 23% had a HR policy.

4.1.4 Number of Staff Lost in the Last 2 Years:

92% of facilities, according to their Administrators, have lost a minimum of 5 staff each in the past two years. Bearing in mind the time and cost of training these health professionals, this trend becomes somewhat alarming, and though 50% of the administrators admit to conducting exit interviews for staff who leave, it is yet to be determined how far what is heard from outgoing staff is used in influencing further action on the issue.

4.2 CURRENT STAFF CATEGORY

4.2.1 Age/Gender Distribution:

The current workforce constitutes mostly of those between the ages of 31 and 40, and majority of them female(63%). Of the 63 current staff interviewed 12 came from accounts, doctors were 7, lab scientists were 8 while nurses were 7. The staff distribution seemed to be one with competence mainly for basic health care.

4.2.2 Number of Years of Work:

Of these numbers only 32.26% have worked for more than five years in the facilities. 45.16% have worked for more than a year but not more than three years while 12% have worked for more than three years.

4.2.3 Career Development:

When asked whether the facilities had a career development plan for staff, 27% were neutral, 25 % agreed, while 38% disagreed. On the other hand majority of staff agreed that staff contribution was appreciated by management of facilities. When asked however whether they considered their workload fair with regards to salary, only 11% agreed. When we add the percentages of those who disagree with those who strongly disagree, we realize that 77% of staff admit that they are over worked, compared to the salaries they receive.

4.2.4 Those on the Verge of Leaving:

It was alarming to realize that in the present workforce there was a huge number considering leaving the services of the facilities. Only 19% considered not leaving at all, and of the 79% that thought of leaving, majority(89%) considered better advancement opportunities as the reason, with better salary following closely. It should be noted that better advancement opportunities also imply better salaries. If this is aggregated it would be seen that issues affecting the job hold the greater leverage influencing staff attrition

(173.10%) than such non-job related issues as location and family reasons(33.34%).

4.2.5 Factors Influencing Staff Who Remain:

It is interesting to note that staff who remain value such aspects as training opportunities, team spirit, loyalty to the community. The respondents mostly were from facilities that had links with donor funded programs which have several training opportunities. For instance the SUSTAIN program managed by CCFN organizes different kinds of programs for clinical staff of facilities. Only 11.11% considered good salary the reason for retaining their services in their present facilities.

FactorsinfluencingToRemain	Frequency	Percent
Training opportunities	28	44.44 %
Team Spirit	28	44.44 %
Your loyalty to the community	26	41.27 %
Others (Specify)	25	39.68 %
Relevance to hospital	23	36.51 %
Work hours or shift	20	31.75 %
Good Hospital Leadership	13	20.63 %
Peer relations	11	17.46 %
Family Ties (e.g. Marriage)	9	14.29 %
Good Salary	7	11.11 %

Staying to benefit from due promotion	4	6.35 %
Retirement benefits	3	4.76 %
Welfare Package (e.g. 13th month salary, leave allowance, reduced hospital bills)	1	1.59

4.3 FORMER STAFF CATEGORY

4.3.1 Age/Gender

This category was made up of about 33 identified and contacted persons. Of this number ,49% were in the age bracket of 21-30 years, reflective of the fact that younger age brackets are more on the move and less ready to accept conditions which they perceive as unfavourable, compared to older age group who may be less critical. 67% were female; this is not surprising as generally women seem to make a greater percentage of the health workforce.

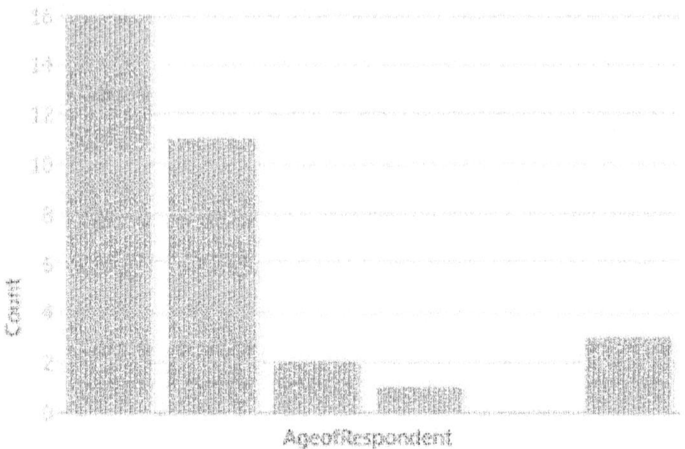

Age

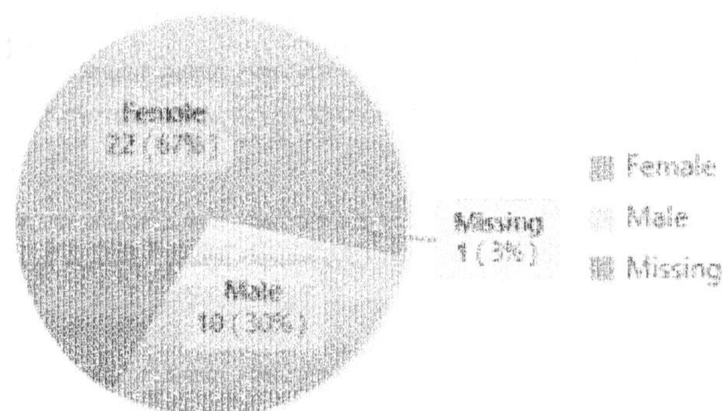

4.3.2 Career Pattern

In terms of professional distribution of staff who have left, majority were in the nursing profession, closely followed by medical doctors. These categories of medical professionals seem generally to be of higher demand. Pharmacists and laboratory scientists then come behind.

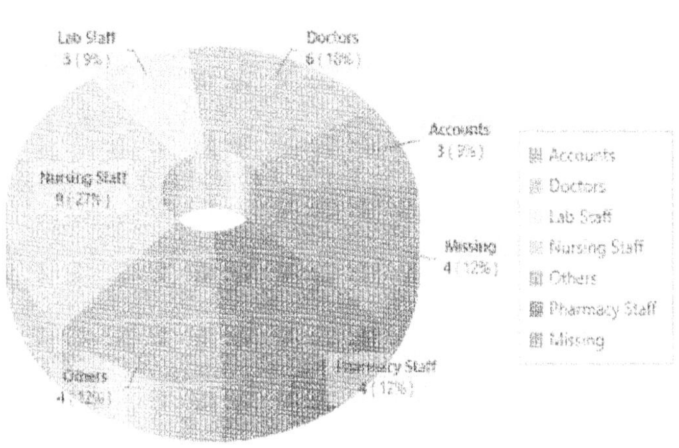

Among all the categories none seemed to have worked for more than three years in the facilities.

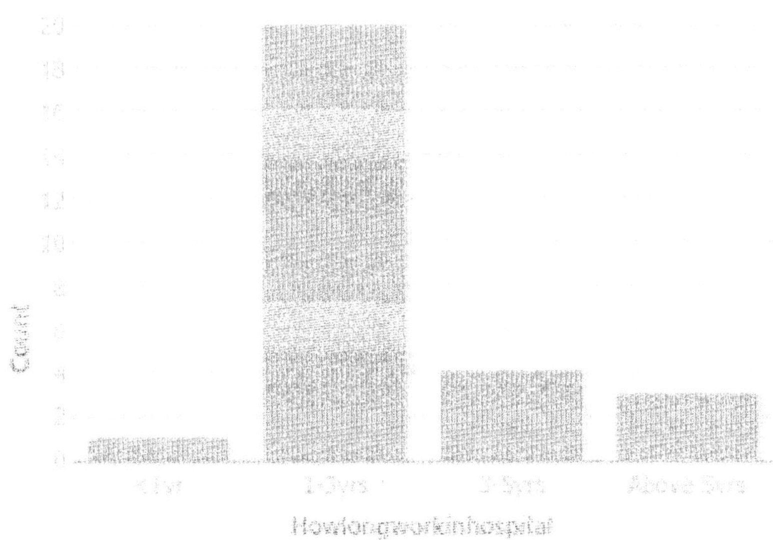

It is significant to note that 24% of those who left still did so even when they did not have other work opportunities.
(Fig….).

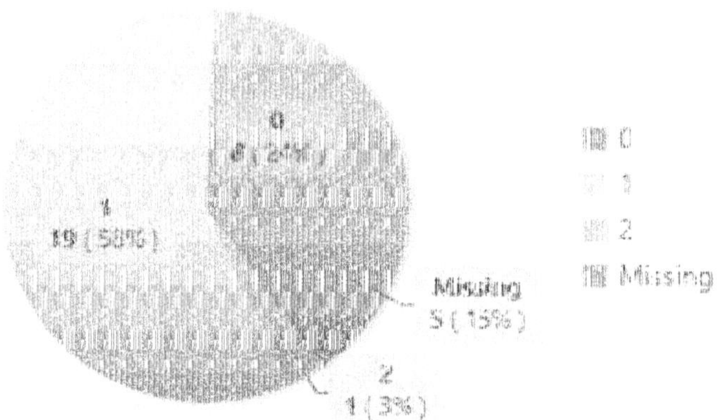

17 of the 33 ex-staff interviewed admitted that career opportunities were limited and was a principal cause of their leaving. Of the total number interviewed, 72% disagree that the workload was fair and commensurate with salaries, with 18% of this figure strongly disagreeing.

Factorsmadeyouleave	Frequency	Percent
Others (Specify)	15	45.45 %
Poor Benefits package	15	45.45 %
Insufficient Training Opportunities	10	30.30 %
Lack of Promotional Opportunities	9	27.27 %
Poor Retirement Package	5	15.15 %
Poor Hospital Leadership	5	15.15 %
Inconvenient work hours or shift	3	9.09 %

Poor Team Spirit	2	6.06 %
Inadequate Workplace Safety	0	0.00 %

On factors that caused them to leave, 45% attributed them to poor benefits package, including a further 15.15% who specifically identified poor or lack of retirement packages. It is interesting to note that 30% identified lack of training opportunities as a cause of leaving; this is surprising being that those who stayed back acknowledged that the availability of training opportunities was partly responsible for their retention. More likely those who gave this reason were ex-staff in non-clinical areas for whom donor driven programs made little or no provision for their continuous training.

5. 0 **SUMMARY OF KEY FINDINGS**

- 54% of the facilities do not have HR unit/officer and only 25% have a HR policy or HR plan

- 84.6% of the hospitals have lost more than 5 staff each over the past 2 years

- 77% of current work force respondents (disagree and strongly disagree) do not believe that their workload is fair and realistic compared to their salary

- 24% of the respondents (former staff) that left the hospitals actually did not have any job offer before leaving

- 63% of respondents (former staff) agreed that they would accept the same job again if they were paid a higher salary
- The most significant factor why staff left was poor benefits package (45%)
- 79% of current staff have thought of leaving
- The main reason for current staff to want to leave is better/advancement opportunities
- The most significant factors influencing staff to stay is training opportunities and team spirit in the hospital (44% each)

6. 0 ROOT CAUSE ANALYSIS :

6.1 Why Why Why ?

If one were to ask the question, why a facility budget does not have a robust allocation for staff benefits, whereas studies have shown that in many countries up to 65 to 80% of health budget is towards human resources for health?[1,2] If one were to ask the reason for the non-compensatory burnouts, one would attribute it of course to the paucity of resources. The scarcity of funds itself is attributable to the fact that end users of faith based facilities strongly believe that services must be free of charge and may evolve all kinds of schemes to not pay their bills even if they could afford them. Most may be genuinely poor. Most faith based facilities themselves have no subvention from government or from anywhere else, and their religious mission disinclines them from taking drastic action against defaulters. Even when they have to charge fees, they charge low fees which do not add up to adequate resources that retain quality staff. Less qualified staff may be employed and trained to take up roles, and as soon as the trained staff see new opportunities, they leave, which becomes a vicious cycle.

When we go down to issues concerning absence of good HRH policies and practices the matter goes beyond financial resources. All the issues could boil down to the perception of facility policy makers and those who plan at the strategic level; the perception that these are faith based facilities and exist in a world of their own. This could either influence things for the better or for worse. In other words there seems to be low sense of competitiveness and an easy acceptance of the status quo which could easily translate to mediocrity. A basic requirement of what one may term comparable excellence is therefore needed to drive change.

Comparable excellence is the ability to maximize one's mission through use of standard systems, processes , appropriate technologies and available opportunities for strategic advantage. While the direct intention is not competition, the sustainable transformation is such that one becomes a preferred option for services. This requires a lot of visioning and intentionality, not waiting to be acted upon by circumstances. An analysis of the weaknesses and threats and a purposeful plan to offset them while chasing the opportunities in a strategic way will be the way to address the issues. A great opportunity exists with the National Health Act. The Act by law makes basic health care the right of all

Nigerians[3]. 50% of funds accrued from funding sources for this act will be used to support eligible providers through the National Health Insurance Scheme[4]. Although eligibility needs to be clearly defined, it is an opportunity for the Church to cash in. 15% of the funds would be used for renovations, while 20% will be used for essential drug procurement. A principal way in which the ordinary person would benefit would be through health insurance for all. If the Church could position herself to provide quality services through her facilities, a huge clientele could be built and there would be no more cases of people defaulting on their bills. Luckily the Church in Nigeria has a health management organization(HMO) called Salus Trust. If Salus Trust could position itself adequately it could have enough leverage to be subscribed with NHIS; this in itself would resolve many financial issues. The National Health Act also makes it illegal to charge fees before treatment during emergencies. 5% of funds are set aside to fund health emergencies[5] . This means that many facilities would be able to make claims and receive payment for cases which they would sometimes have let go in the past because of stubborn defaulters. It waits to be seen how this provision would be respected by Nigerian service providers who have a tendency to exploit weak monitoring systems.

7.0 SOME RECOMMENDATIONS:

Based on the foregoing, the following recommendations are made:

1.   Realizing that basic health is a right, it is not the duty of the Church to provide health care but government's and therefore resort to an aggressive advocacy with government at all levels using data generated from health facilities, especially data that show access and default payment is necessary. The idea here is to show that there is demand for health care services provided by church facilities, and inadequate financial capacity by end users to pay for services. The Church should explore the provisions in the Health Act that "The Federal Ministry, any state ministry or any Local Government or any public health establishment may enter into an agreement with any private practitioner, private health establishment or non-governmental organization in order to achieve any objective of this Act."[6] The church should leverage its long history of health care services to enter into MOUs that have staff seconded from government, where grants-in-aid for renovations, maintenance and equipment are provided by government.

2.   Fatith based organisations should strategically locate themselves to benefit from the provision of the basic health care through insurance in the National Health Act. This would come in the form of best practices that stand out the facilities.

3.   Faith based organisations should realize that fees alone cannot provide needed resources for health care; therefore generating support through annual appeals to high net

worth individuals and church wide appeals when people congregate are important fundraising steps.

4. Faith based facilities should drive the demand for health care services through community outreaches. Using the ecclesiastical structures, regular outreaches could increase uptake, as most poor populations hardly go to health facilities unless they are helplessly ill. In this vein investing in mobile diagnostic services would go a long way.

5. Faith based health facilities should strive to remain preferred options for end users through affectionate care and genuine drug dispensing. Ethical issues and dry compassion associated with facilities in the public sector should not be found within them.

6. A strategic plan for human resources for health and setting down Human Resource policies that are standard are important steps. There are sample policies that could be adapted and domesticated. Policies are not meant for government agencies or big private corporations but are a way in which an institution is set and run.

7. Ensure facility budgets have proper allocative and operational efficiency.[7] It could so happen sometimes that despite the low fees, a well located faith based facility shows enough surplus in its balance sheet, often such surplus is as a result of poor allocation for human resources. When tax authorities look at the books, they demand for tax, whereas they are not-for-profit institutions.

Faith based health facilities should strive to pay their staff better than government, if possible.

8. Eschew mediocrity: A mindset that anything goes should be fervently discouraged. Although G.K. Chesterton had said that anything worth doing was worth doing badly, meaning that if something had to be done anyway, it should be done no matter the outcome, nevertheless healthcare provision is a serious service which should not be allowed to suffer mediocrity. Standard of hygiene and practice should be set and monitored for compliance.

8.0 Conclusion: The recommendations set out below are common sense recommendations. The principles could be applied by church actors across a broad spectrum of social services. The church is an expert in the provision of social services and therefore should leverage this expertise. In a context where the Sustainable Development Goals(SDGs) have already been adopted, the need to put these recommendations into practice becomes urgent and important. Goal 3 of the SDGs seeks to ensure healthy lives and promote well-being for all at all ages, and has such targets as reducing maternal mortality to less than 70 per 100,000, ending preventable deaths of newborns to as low as 12 per 1000 births, and ending the AIDS epidemic, tuberculosis, malaria and neglected tropical diseases as well communicable diseases such as hepatitis, among other targets. The church could play an important role in meeting these targets, motivated by her quest for the wellbeing and salvation of the whole person.

Acknowledgements

I sincerely acknowledge the assistance of Justin Ekpa, John Olawepo, *John Oko, 'Wale Fadare , Dotun Omitayo, Roland Mordi , Margaret Erhabor, Justin Ekpa, John Olawepo, Florence Okakwu, Grace Okoye and those who visited the field.*

REFERENCES

1. *Kolehamainen-Aiken RL:* ***Decentralization and human resources: implications and impact.****Human Resources for Health Development Journal 1997,* **2(1):***1-14.*

2. *Saltman RB, Von Otter C: Implementing Planned Markets in Health Care: Balancing Social and Economic Responsibility. Buckingham: Open University Press; 1995.*

3. *National Health Bill Art. 1(e), 3(3)*

4. *National Health Bill Art. 11 (3a)*

5. *National Health Bill Art. 11 (3e)*

6. *National Health Bill Art. 18(2)*

"In assessing the financing of human resources for health it is important to evaluate whether the funding is being used efficiently...whether the salaries are the producing the highest levels of services for the funding(operational efficiency); and

whether the salaries are the right thing to be funding for achieving health objectives(allocative efficiency)." Thomas Bossert et al : Assessing Financing, Education, Management and Policy Context for Strategic Planning of Human Resources for Health. World Health Organization 2007, 22.

CHAPTER EIGHT

CATHOLIC SOCIAL TEACHING AND HUMAN EXPLOITATION:
A REFLECTION ON THE OCCASION OF THE COATNET MEETING IN PARIS, FRANCE ON THE 9TH OF NOVEMBER 2015

Introduction:

The phenomenon of human exploitation primarily springs from a lack of universalizing the concept of the inherent dignity of the human person. The abuse and exploitation of other human beings by better privileged or more powerful persons is as old as human society itself. Take a look at our history; when did we have the Universal Declaration of Human Rights? Only in 1948. When was racial segregation removed in public facilities and institutions in the United States? Only with the 1964 Civil Rights Act, although there was an earlier ruling in 1954 banning segregation in public schools. When did Blacks actually start voting in the United States? It should have been since 1870 but it was only with the Voting Rights Act of 1965 that all the hurdles were removed and Blacks could vote unhindered. Or when did Apartheid end in South Africa? After a little more than three years of negotiation beginning in 1990, it effectively ended in 1994 with the general elections won by African National Congress. **It seems more true to say that the tolerance for human exploitation has been far longer in our various cultures than the consciousness for universal recognition of the intrinsic worth and value of every human person**. I am not even mentioning the centuries of inter-ethnic wars in Africa, the caste systems in India, the slavery and the transatlantic slave trade that took place in the past.

In spite of all the safeguards and the legislations put in place in our contemporary world, human beings are still exploiting the labour of other human beings in unsafe work conditions and wages that are a poor opposite of the human energy exerted; in Nigeria, Chinese companies exploit workers in unsafe conditions; in plantations in Gabon, people work as if they are slaves; in Dubai, we hear of the bonded labour that builds the city; and in many parts of Nigeria, children are brought in from other countries as domestic helps and suffer all kinds of abuses; and there is the trafficking in human persons for sexual exploitation which is now a multi-billion dollar business. The most tragic human exploitation is poor governance and failure of government that exists in many countries of the world, leading to terrorism, extreme poverty and a migration crisis which has left many corpses in the dessert and in the oceans, as young men and women struggle to seek for green pastures. Pope Francis acknowledged this during his address at the UN when he challenged the political will of leaders of governments to put an end "to the phenomenon of social and economic exclusion, with its baneful consequences: human trafficking, the marketing of human organs and tissues, the sexual exploitation of boys and girls, slave labour, including prostitution, the drug and weapons trade, terrorism and international organised crime."

Another angle is the phenomenon of self-trafficking, with many young women willingly offering themselves for sexual exploitation in Europe. Some arrive in Europe pregnant, struggle to gain citizenship for their children, and stay back to be integrated in the European society or engage in sex trade.

Social Teaching and the Gap of Conscientization

Beyond the safeguards and the legislations put in place by various governments to overcome human exploitation and promote the idea of universal consciousness of the dignity of every human being, there is a gap of a philosophical and theological bases which the Social Teaching does fill. Government can enforce its laws and individuals and groups could seek redress, but more importantly we have to engage in an education of conscience which would free the individual and dignify him or her and his or her circle of relationships. Pope Francis has reiterated the fact that "Integral human development and the full exercise of human dignity cannot be imposed. They must be built up and allowed to unfold for each individual, for every family, in communion with others, and in a right relationship with all those areas in which human social life develops – friends, communities, towns and cities, schools, businesses and unions, provinces, nations, etc."(UN Address); the Holy Father acknowledges that this cannot take place without the right to an education which has the family as the centre piece.

Dignity and Solidarity: A consciousness of right to dignity must of necessity be in conjunction with the demand for solidarity otherwise we have the extreme of individualism. In Evangeli Vitae, Pope St. John Paul points out that " the roots of the contradiction between the solemn affirmation of human rights and their tragic denial in practice lies in a notion of freedom which exalts the isolated individual in an absolute way, and gives no place to solidarity, to openness to others and service of them..." (no. 19). Solidarity therefore ensures that while one is educated to be conscious of his or her own dignity, this is extended in an active way to others, expressed in a deep passion that translates into action that dignifies or seeks to dignify others. In Solicitudo Rei Socialis St. John Paul says "Solidarity is not a feeling of vague compassion or shallow distress at the misfortunes of so many people, both near and far. On the contrary, it is a firm and persevering determination to commit oneself to the common good; that is to say, to the good of all and of each individual, because we are all really responsible for all."(no.38).

The sense of solidarity and the common good should fuel the drive for elimination of inequalities and exploitation. Pope Francis has pointed out that this is not possible without a mental conversion. In Evangelii Gaudium, he says if we do not believe in the universal destination of goods and see solidarity as restoring to the poor what belongs to them, even if we put structures in place, they would eventually become "corrupt, ineffectual and oppressive"(no.189). A mental attitude which is as a result of a good education of conscience is very important.

The Social Teaching are quite relevant in this mental conversion. Beginning from Rerum Novarum they have critically analysed the human condition but beyond that, they have created a better understanding of humanity and made actual proposals to improve on it. Take the question of labour. Almost every social encyclical has dealt with labour. Laborem Exercens especially gives an excellent understanding. It draws attention to the human being as the subject of work and that we should consider the subject more valuable than the object of work. Looking only at the objective value led in the past to categorizing people into different classes, where people who engaged in work that demanded physical exertion were seen in lower categories. Laborem Exercens argues that the fact that Jesus, 'while being God, became like us in all things devoted most of the years of his life on earth to manual work in the carpenter's bench,'(no.6), transformed the concept of work. What is therefore more important is the subject of work, which is always the human being. Work is a means of fulfilling the vocation to be a human person. Work is 'for us' and not we 'for work'.(ibid). In this sense dignity is not in the kind of work but in the fact that whatever work is being done is by a human person.(ibid). The phrase 'there is dignity in labour' derives from this understanding, that every aspect of work matters not in terms of its objectivity but in the sense that the subject of it is a human being. It thus brings about a general de-classification, as human beings are not to be positioned based on the kind of work they do but by the fact that all work has value because the one undertaking it has inherent value. This inherent value should determine the wage bill. In this sense it goes on to propose what is called Family Wage, where no matter how menial work is, the wages should take care of the needs of one's family. We must not forget though that what we mean by work must be something of positive value. Armed robbery, human trafficking, prostitution cannot be seen as work. Laborem Exercens goes on to raise the issue of unemployment as beyond an economic factor but an anthropological factor, because work helps the human being to have meaning.

The church can only do so much, because she is mother and teacher. She is not an alternate government. She has offered the Social Teaching to the world, and it is the duty of everyone to take it and spread it. By and large I think the concerns of the Social Teaching over the years are now captured as an action plan by the world, with the 2030 Sustainable Development agenda.

The SDGs and the Common Good

For me, the SDGs encapsulate the concerns of the Social Teaching with regard to dignifying the human condition. The SDGs make the hope which the church has repeatedly expressed about human solidarity, possible. Imagine if world leaders took the call of Pope Francis seriously to desist from a 'declarational nominalism' and make real effort to implement the SDGs! it would certainly contribute towards realizing the vision of a better world as captured in the SDG document. Let me quote some sections of this vision:

We envisage a world of universal respect for human rights and human dignity, the rule of law, justice, equality and non-discrimination; of respect for race, ethnicity and cultural diversity; and of equal opportunity permitting the full realization of human potential and contributing to shared prosperity. A world which invests in its children and in which every child grows up free from violence and exploitation. A world in which every woman and girl enjoys full gender equality and all legal, social and economic barriers to their empowerment have been removed. A just, equitable, tolerant, open and socially inclusive world in which the needs of the most vulnerable are met.

The SDGs offer great hope of transforming our world and reducing the exploitation of human beings. As Flintoff (2002) has said, "the key thing is not to make despair convincing but to make hope possible." (Flintoff, J. How to Change the World, 2002. P.69). We have to buy into this agenda and promote it as the framework for development. As Pope Paul Vl said in Populorum Progressio,"*the development of peoples has the Church's close attention, particularly the development of those peoples who are striving to escape from hunger, misery, endemic disease and ignorance; of those who are looking for a wider share in the benefits of civilization and a more active improvement of their human qualities; of those who are aiming purposefully at their complete fulfillment.*" (no.1).

CHAPTER NINE

THE CHURCH AND TAXATION: AN ADVISORY FOR DIOCESAN AND RELIGIOUS INSTITUTIONS IN NIGERIA

With Maria Nkese Udonwo

1.0 Introduction

These guidelines disclose the Nigerian tax laws and regulations with respect to charitable and not-for-profit organisations in Nigeria. They aim at enlightening the Church Diocesan and Religious institutions on their rights and obligations under the Nigerian tax law.

The guidelines start with the relationship of the Catholic Diocesan and Religious institutions to charitable and non-profit organisations (CNPOs). It highlights some relevant categories of taxation in Nigeria, and the duties/obligations of Church institutions under the tax laws, even though they may have tax exemption approval. It concludes with a recommendation for the Church's Diocesan and Religious institutions in Nigeria to comply with the tax laws and regulations of the land.

2. 0 Background

The Catholic Church agencies in Nigeria, such as the diocesan and religious institutions are classified under the Nigerian tax law as charitable and private non-profit organisations (CPNPOs) because they play a significant role in undertaking a shared responsibility for the social and developmental needs of the society. These institutions, registered either as trustee or a company limited by guarantee, are tax exempt when operating within the ambit of their Memorandum and Articles of Association or Constitution. However, they are brought under various tax obligations when they indulge in commercial activities or make payments to taxable individuals/organisations.

The growing demand on non-profit organisations to provide goods and services which the government cannot or will not fund put religious and diocesan institutions on the pathway of commercial activities, therefore making these hitherto tax exempt institutions liable to the payment of income tax on the commercial activities they undertake. It should be noted that when charitable and non-profit organisations engage in profit making ventures outside the legal objects of their establishment, they become subject to taxation and could have their tax exemption approvals revoked in some instances. There is therefore a need for public disclosure reporting and filing of annual returns to ensure transparency, accountability, due diligence checks and make for proper monitoring and control.

3. 0 Taxation in Nigeria

Taxation in Nigeria is enforced by the three tiers of government: Federal, State and Local Government, with each tier having its approved list of collections as found in the Taxes and Levies Decree 1998.

The taxes collected by the Federal Government that are of relevance to us include Company Income Tax; Withholding Tax; Value Added Tax; Personal Income Tax (for Abuja residents); Capital Gains Tax(for Abuja residents and corporate bodies); and Stamp Duties (for corporate entities).

Among the taxes collected by the State Governments are Personal Income Tax (PAYE), Capital Gains Tax (CGT), Stamp Duties and Business Premises Registration.

The Local Government collect Registration fees for births, marriages and deaths; signage/advertisement fees; tenement rates; waste disposal; burial ground and religious places permit among others.

4. 0 Taxation and the Activities of Charitable and Private Non-Profit Organisation

Section 23, subsection (c) of the Company Income Tax Act exempts the income/profits of NGOs derived from ecclesiastical, charitable or educational activities of a public character from tax. These income/profits are presumed to accrue from grants and donations and should be for the performance of some forms of public duty. It is important for Church institutions to register with Federal Inland Revenue Service (FIRS) in order to obtain a Tax Identification Number (TIN) using their certificate of incorporation, constitution/memorandum of Association, business address and commencement date. This registration enables the CPNPO to apply to the Tax Exempt Unit (TEU) of FIRS for tax exemption certificate. It should be noted however, that tax exemption does not discharge the CPNPO from tax obligations such as Pay-As-You-Earn (PAYE), Value Added Tax (VAT), Capital Gains Tax (CGT) or Withholding Tax (WHT).

Where the organisation engages in trade or business in addition to the public duties it carries out, then, that part of the income from trade or business is subject to tax under the Company Income Tax Act (CITA). According to Section 55, subsection 1 of CITA, it is mandatory for every organisation, including those granted tax exemption, to file a self-assessment tax returns with FIRS at least once a year.

5. 0 Duties of Charitable and Private Non-Profit Organisation

It is the duty of diocesan and religious institutions which are classified as CPNPOs under the Nigerian Tax laws to:

- Register with Tax Authority for tax purposes
- Serve as an agent of collection for PAYEE, WHT and VAT
- Register with PAYE in line with the PAYE regulation
- Deduct PAYE from staff income and remit to tax authority on or before the 10th day of the following month
- Deduct and remit WHT on third party transactions
- Pay Capital Gains Tax on sales of organisation's property
- Request and confirm evidence of tax payment from third parties when entering into contract with them
- Keep adequate records and books of transactions
- File in Employers Annual Returns in line with the provisions of Section 81 of PITA
- File Annual Tax Returns in line with Provisions of Section 55 of CITA

6. 0 Relevant Tax Regulations in Nigeria for Charitable and Private Non-Profit Organisation

6. 1 Personal Income Tax

Personal income tax (PIT), also known as Pay-As-You-Earn (PAYE), is the tax liable on the aggregate income of a taxpayer, be it salaries, wages, fees, allowances or other gains/benefits. In Nigeria, it is the duty of the employer of labour to act as the agent of the tax authority in deducting this tax from employees at source, and remitting same to the relevant tax office.

The residency determines the extent of the taxpayer's tax liability. A person is deemed to be resident in Nigeria if s/he resides for 183 days in any 12 month period in the country. However, a Nigerian resident permit holder is liable to pay tax in Nigeria whether or not s/he resides in the country for less than 183 days in 12 months. Personal income tax should be remitted to the relevant tax authority in the territory of the taxpayer's principal place of business or residence.

Items exempted from PIT include: Medical/dental expenses; gratuities and severance compensation; interests on loans for owner-occupier residential house; Leave allowance (10% of annual basic salary subject to a maximum of ₦7,500).

Though religious bodies do not pay tax, this does not mean that those under their employ do not. Staff in schools, hospitals, facilities run by religious bodies, have to pay PAYE and it is the responsibility of the management of those institutions to work their PAYE out and pay to government; and if religious persons earn an income in the course of their work they pay tax from it. Unfortunately priests who serve in parishes hardly have a stated income and depend largely on the charity of the members. However if a diocese were to structure the emolument of the priests and pay them salaries, diocesan authorities would need to work out the PAYE.

6. 2 Withholding Tax

Withholding tax is an advance tax payment deducted at source from the income of a taxpayer on account of the ultimate income tax liability of that taxpayer or company. It started in Nigeria in 1977 as part of the first tax reforms aimed at addressing the challenge of tax evasion.

Sections 78 to 81 of CITA mandates all persons, including charitable and private non-profit organisations (CPNPOs), to withhold tax on certain transactions such as rent, interest and all forms of contract, and remit same to the relevant tax authority on or before the 21st day of the month following the month that payment was made for those transactions. This means that persons not liable to pay tax are obligated to deduct withholding tax from payments that are tax deductible.

Deductions of Withholding tax could be on payments for contracts; supplies; commissions; consultancy, professional and management services; technical services; agency arrangement; building, construction and related activities; director's fees; rent; interests, royalty and dividends. Applicable WHT rates vary from 5% to 10%, depending on the type of payment being made and the paying entity (corporate or individual).

6. 2. 1 Rates of WHT :

The applicable rates of WHT are as follows:

Types of payment	Applicable rates for	
	Companies	Individual
Dividends, Interest, Rent	10%	10%
Directors Fees	10%	10%
Royalties	15%	15%
Commission, Consultation, Technical, Service Fees	10%	5%
Management fees	10%	5%
Construction/Building Contracts	5%	5%
Contracts, other than outright sales		
and purchase of goods in the ordinary course of business	5%	5%

WHT deduction is not an additional cost of contract, supply or service to be added to the price; rather, it is the tax due on payment. The deduction is remitted to Federal Inland Revenue

Service (FIRS) and the tax payer issued a tax invoice. The taxpayer may use the tax withheld to set-off tax liabilities that may be due to such income. It is paid in the name of the person or company whose tax has been withheld.

6. 2. 2. Penalty for Late or Non-Remittance of Withholding Tax

All withholding tax liabilities are required to be collected and paid over to the tax authorities within 30 days of their becoming due for payment. The time within which taxes withheld are to be remitted has been reduced from 30 to 21 days for Companies as per the Companies Income Tax Amendments Act 2007. Where there is a failure to remit this Tax for whatever reason, the penalty on conviction is a 200% fine of the tax due in addition to commercial rates of interest until the entire amount accessed as withholding tax is fully paid.

7. 0 Value Added Tax (VAT)

Value added tax is a multi-stage tax imposed on goods and services through the various stages in the production and distribution chain.

Nigeria operates a low flat rate of 0% and 5% on all VAT able goods and services. Zero-rating means that those goods/services are taxed at zero percentage. Of importance to Catholic Diocesan and Religious institutions is that, goods purchased for use in humanitarian donor-funded projects and imports by registered non-profit organisations fall under one of the categories of zero-rated transactions because these activities are not for profit purposes and as such, exempted from VAT. These institutions are therefore eligible for VAT refund on their local purchases (goods and services), imports and foreign aided projects upon request and submission of a completed form and the required documentary evidence as prescribed by FIRS.

It should however be noted that these charities and non-profit organisations are obligated in line with the provisions of the law to file VAT returns to the tax authority, otherwise face a penalty of Five Thousand Naira (₦5000) only, for every month in which the failure continues.

All CPNPOs are encouraged to register as agents of FIRS for the purpose of VAT collection, deduct VAT from source before making payments to contractors/suppliers, issue tax invoices for goods/services rendered and remit same to the nearest FIRS office on or before the 21st day of the month following that in which the transaction occurred, as well as maintain records of all VAT transactions.

8. 0 Capital Gains Tax

Capital Gains Tax (CGT) pertains to all gains accruing to a taxpayer from the sale or lease or other transfer of proprietary rights, on tangible or intangible assets situated within or outside Nigeria, in a chargeable interest. CGT accrues on an actual year basis at a rate of 10%.

Computation of capital gains tax is done by deducting from the sum received or receivable, the cost of acquisition to the person realizing the chargeable gain plus expenditure incurred on the improvement or expenses incidental to the realization of the asset.

9. 0 A Few Recommendations:

In the light of the pressure being mounted in some quarters for religious bodies to pay tax; for instance the Religious Committee of the National Dialogue/Conference, resolved that religious bodies should pay tax, although this was highly disparaged, it is important to note that the FIRS may want to throw more searchlight on allied institutions such as Health Centres, Clinics, Hospitals, schools, that are owned and run by the Church. FIRS is under severe pressure to beef up the tax regime, especially in the light of low oil earnings, and as it appears that those in the tax service earn certain commissions arising from performance, officials may continue the lobby for the church to pay tax, in order to enlarge their portfolios. Church paying tax may amount to changing the law and regulations concerning not-for-profits, which may mean that donations would fall under the axe of the tax man. This may seem a difficult nut for government to crack so we need not be worried about this.

Many church are being intimidated by tax authorities to pay taxes on schools run by them, forgetting that there is a provision in the Companies Income Tax Act (CITA) section 23(1) (c) exempting a *"company engaged in ecclesiastical, charitable or educational activities of a public character from tax provided that such activities are not derived from a trade or business carried on by the company."* In other words, so long as the establishment of schools and their running is not done through a trade or business carried out by the church, tax is not to be paid by the school no matter the surpluses; rather the surpluses are used to develop infrastructure, pay staff well who pay their taxes, etc.

Traditionally institutions such as hospitals, schools, nursing homes, old people's homes etc have been part of the mandate of the church, providing services for the poor in hard to reach areas, and in many instances being the only available means of service. Using her skilled religious personnel to run some of these institutions, the church has managed to maintain them through thick and thin without huge administrative costs. While there may be a few far flung cases of government grant-in-aid as in Anambra State, the overall situation is that these institutions have to struggle on their own to remain afloat and so affordable fees may be charged.

The Church needs to assert its stand as a not-for-profit entity and prove that even when fees are charged, it is not so as the left over would be shared among the owners of the institution or facility, but is consistently and faithfully ploughed back into making the institution better and offsetting other associated costs. Not-for-profit does not mean that one operates at a loss, but whatever income that accrues is not shared among the Trustees but used in furthering the objects of the entity, which in this case, is the Church's mission.

There are insinuations that some of these institutions have departed from their main objects of non-profit services to profit making entities in terms of huge balances in their ledgers after all expenditures.   There are insinuations of fees that are not commensurate with the services offered, poor staff attitude and low motivation. Tax authorities would only be delighted to examine the books of such institutions and take a chunk into the coffers of government with the excuse that they are fee collecting services and not necessarily donations. The Church however must stand firm in her explanations about her not-for-profit status and the fact that no money is shared out to anyone, as directors and shareholders of profit making entities would do.

Yet in truth these balances exist because there is inadequate utilization of resources and because many areas are left to suffer paucity. For instance some of these facilities suffer severe dilapidation, are run with extremely frugal application of resources, and staff are very poorly paid. A hefty balance in the midst of run down infrastructure and low salaries is not profit, it is poor stewardship.

Dioceses could improve stewardship by ensuring the following:

1. Have a consolidated diocesan annual budget that factors in all income from pastoral, health and educational institutions and allocate resources appropriately. This means the diocese should be treated as a whole, except where certain institutions are separately registered with the Corporate Affairs Commission; the chancery should reflect their budgets in the overall diocesan budget. Areas of shortfall should be replenished by areas of overflow. The running costs of the Bishop's house and his Chancery, part of the salaries of staff could be part of the expenses of these income generating facilities, as the Bishop and Chancery serve the entire diocese. This way there is less pressure on income that is generated through gifts and donations.

2. In making the capital budget of the diocese, it should be possible to use resources from these institutions to develop infrastructure in less endowed areas so that at the end of each year there is reflected a more comprehensive use of resources.

3. Establish a Human Resources policy that factors in the concern of *Rerum Novarum* and *Laborem Exercens* for a living wage. The issue of tax payment by the church(institutions) provides an opportunity to various dioceses to consider more compassionately what they pay to church workers. Assuming the church were to pay tax, the question to address theoretically is whether it is better to give away this money to government or to use it to pay staff properly. Of course it would be much better to pay workers properly, as the workers would themselves pay PAYE tax to government. The Catholic Secretariat of Nigeria agencies have demonstrated that one could work in the church and be paid competitively. The CBCN as a Conference has been quite proactive on this note as well as many other areas. Diocesan institutions need to follow suit. The church as an institution of charity may even opt to pay

better salaries than government, assuming our institutions generate enough resources for this. If diocesan institutions pay competitive salaries this could lead to better staff motivation and greater productivity. Other benefits for staff could include health insurance, pension contribution, National Housing Fund etc.

4. Establish an endowment Fund, with contributions from all the institutions.

5. Support JDPC/Caritas: Use funds from these income generating sources to support the advocacy efforts, the charity and welfare, and emergency response initiatives of the church.

6. Have a reserve fund: A reserve fund serves the purposes of meeting needs during critical situations. Strict regulations could be made with regard to accessing these funds so they truly remain for the rainy day. The biting effect of drop in oil prices in the overall economy was because Nigeria as a nation did not save enough for the rainy day.

The church could never make profit, because there are a thousand and one things that always require the use of resources. This does not mean however that the church cannot have good balances in accounts. Funds, so long as they come from donations and gifts are not taxable and the Diocese could save excess income in a reserve fund. If government turns around in the future to tax churches, what this would mean is that even funds from donations, gifts, would be taxed; this would also require government to change the law concerning the status of not for profit organisations, as we have mentioned above. This is not likely to happen, for all over the world there is a recognition of the not- for- profit sector which the church is a major part of. Nevertheless diocesan institutions should learn to make proper use of resources that come from allied institutions to fulfill the mission of the church.

10.0 Conclusion

These guidelines highlight the rights and duties of Catholic Diocesan and Religious institutions as charitable and private non-profit organisations (CPNPOs) under the provisions of the Nigerian Tax Law. They indicate how these institutions could comply with tax laws and regulations so as to avoid default fines. They outline the different tax heads and how tax exemption approval could be obtained. Charitable and private non-profit organisations (CPNPOs) are urged to collaborate with tax authorities as a moral and statutory responsibility, by registering with relevant tax authorities, serving as tax collection agents (PAYEE, WHT and VAT), remitting same to the relevant tax authorities, filing tax returns and paying taxes when they engage in trade or business activities. It also observes that failure to submit tax returns even by tax exempt organisations would attract a penalty.

The Catholic Church Diocesan and Religious institutions in Nigeria are therefore encouraged to review and streamline their accounting and financial activities to comply with the Nigerian tax laws and regulations. This would not only portray the Church as leading by good example by obeying the legitimate laws of the land, but would avoid attracting sanctions and stiff penalties from the Nigerian Tax Authorities.

REFERENCES:

Ibeabuchi, C. (2012) Religious Bodies, NGOs must Pay Tax for Trading Subsidiaries, FRC insists. Vanguard, Lagos

Lawal, B. T. (2013) The Charitable and Private Non-Profit Organisations in Nigeria and their Tax Obligations, Federal Inland Revenue Service Workshop, Abuja

Olusegun, K.T. (2013) Value Added Tax (VAT) Administration in

Nigeria: The Role of Charitable and Private Non-Profit Organisations, Federal Inland Revenue Service Workshop, Abuja

Oni, I.O. (2008) Nigerian Companies Income Tax (Law and Practice)

Serah, W. (2013) Understanding Withholding Tax (WHT) and the Role of Charitable and Private Non-Profit Organisations in Nigeria, Federal Inland Revenue Service Workshop, Abuja

CHAPTER TEN

MOBILIZING STATE SUPPORT FOR NON STATE ACTORS

1.1 Introduction:

In many different ways, various persons and groups have acknowledged the complimentary role of Civil Society Organisations to government, in the provision of social services to citizens of this great country. Notable areas are in health and education. Various persons also acknowledge the efforts of some conscientious state governments in funding partnerships with the Church. For instance Peter Obi, former governor of Anambra State, Elechi of Ebonyi State etc. Benue has had a long standing relationship as far as funding education is concerned. Recently, at the just concluded plenary meeting of the Catholic Bishops' Conference of Nigeria, the Bishops requested Dr. Goodluck Jonathan to look into the matter of government support for services rendered by voluntary agencies, especially in education.

The question is how could we make this support regular and consistent and justiciable ? How could we replicate ongoing efforts and make them sustainable ? For the truth is that the progress of a society cannot be pinned to the goodwill of a few willing leaders but through established frameworks that force even those without goodwill to have a minimum of responsiveness. As the Vatican Council Fathers said in Justice in the World "In the face of international systems of domination, the bringing about of justice depends more and more on the determined will for development.'(no.1). Paul VI said in Populorum Progressio, "The present situation of the world demands concerted action based on a clear vision of all economic, social, cultural and spiritual aspects.'(no 13). The time for waiting for something to happen is over. The world gave us a great example with the universal declaration of Human Rights in 1948, and gave us another example with the adoption of the Millennium Development Goals in 2000, and continues to give example with the progress of work on the post 2015 Sustainable Development Goals.

Without working to change structures, non-governmental institutions will continue to exhaust themselves in service provision meant really to be the primary work of government. Civil Society needs to continue to identify gaps, proffer solutions, and maintain a consistent strident voice that draws attention to issues, as well as build effective partnerships that would effect change for the good of our people. Whether as service providers or as advocates of change, Civil Society Organisations require funding.

1.2 Commendations From the UNGA Outcome Document

From the outcome Document of the Septemeber 25th 2013 UN general assembly, the Heads of States and Governments had this to say about the MDGS: *'We welcome what has been achieved so far. The Millennium Development Goals have provided a common vision and contributed to remarkable progress. Significant and substantial advances have been made in meeting several of the targets. However, we are concerned at the unevenness and gaps in achievement and at the immense challenges that remain. The MDGs are critical for meeting the basic needs of people in developing countries; as we approach the 2015 deadline, unrelenting efforts are required to accelerate progress across all the Goals.'* (UNGA 2013 Outcome Document) .

It is not in doubt that whatever success that was recorded in implementing the millennium development goals programme would not have come about without the active support of non State actors. The huge gaps remaining to be filled could better be done with the active engagement of the non state sector.

1.21 From Poverty Reduction to Eradication

More than ever before, the Heads of States and governments have recognized the imperative of a universally accepted agenda for development, and seeing how valuable the MDGs are, have made a shift from poverty reduction to a commitment towards the eradication of poverty beyond 2015. The development agenda beyond 2015 has been more participatory with consultations all over the world with CSOs. In our small way we were part of the world wide consultation on behalf of Caritas Internationalis. To implement this commitment to poverty eradication, non State actors especially Civil Society Organisations and Faith Based Organisations are going to be direly needed. Let us quote again from the outcome document:

'We are resolved that the post-2015 development agenda should reinforce the international

community's commitment to poverty eradication and sustainable development. We

underscore the central imperative of poverty eradication and are committed to freeing

humanity from poverty and hunger as a matter of urgency. Recognising the intrinsic

interlinkage between poverty eradication and promotion of sustainable development, we

underline the need for a coherent approach which integrates in a balanced manner the

three dimensions of sustainable development. This coherent approach involves working

towards a single framework and set of Goals -universal in nature and applicable to all

countries, while taking account of differing national circumstances and respecting national

policies and priorities. It should also promote peace and security, democratic governance, the

rule of law, gender equality and human rights for all.'(UNGA Outcome Doc 2013).

1.3 Framework for Support

In view of the complementary role of non State actors in development , we are advocating for a policy measure to be put in place to encourage non State actors to more than ever before partner with government in development. That policy measure is by establishing National Development Fund for Civil Society Organisations.

The fundamental basis for this advocacy is from the Principle of Subsidiarity where a 'higher level of government or organization should not perform any function or duty that can be handled more effectively at a lower level by people who are closer to the problem and have a better understanding of the issue.' This is a pillar of Catholic Social Teaching. (CCFN Handbook). For instance certain non state actors like the church have been working in certain areas like health and education far longer than any government and can do better with support.

The second basis is that funds controlled by government do not belong to government officials but to the people and CSOs serve the people.

The third basis is that it is being done in other countries. This advocacy is important because if issues are not provided a legal framework then they can only depend on the goodwill of those in authority, and good will is not enough. This is why we are holding this discussion. We have held one in Calabar already and have met with a few legislators. We are hoping to be greatly enriched by your participation and hope that this could be something we could put forward together.

1.4 Goal: What would be the goal of this Fund ? It would be to enhance State and peoples partnerships for the promotion of the dignity of the human person. If people access affordable, quality services, their dignity is enhanced.

1.5 Sources of Funds: The source has to be a stable one. In Estonia it is through the national budget. In South Africa it is through the Budget and the Lottery. In Nigeria, a small percentage of the budget could be set aside for this, or since government is always so looking for money, it could come directly from the people through a two percent increase in VAT that is dedicated entirely to this Fund.(Let us reflect on the implications of VAT increase.)

1.6 Structure: This Fund would have a governing board appointed from non state actors and ratified by the national assembly, whose function would be independent of government by statute. All its guiding policies would have to be accessible by all, including minutes of meetings that should be posted on its websites. Clear eligibility criteria will be established for any non State actor that would apply to the Fund; and combined with clear selection criteria, will guide the calls for proposals. International external assessors could be engaged to reassess proposals, and clear mechanisms should exist where complaints could be addressed.

There should also be a mechanism for reporting and evaluation. This can occur at two levels, where the funding a non-state actor has received is assessed to know whether the objective is being met; the second level is when there is periodic evaluation to assess the overall objective of the Fund.

1.7 Truth About Nigerians

I know civil servants will establish NGOs and all such groups overnight and attempt to corrupt the Fund. But the truth about Nigerians is that where something has clear guidelines and criteria, and initial gra-gra fails, Nigerians usually seek ways to do what is required. Those who spoil us are our leaders. People are the same everywhere. There are Nigerians in the UK, US etc, and they are law abiding. All over the world, if allowance is made for abuse, people will abuse, but if there are strict guidelines and criteria even Nigerians obey. If we want we could even approach such agencies as USAID, DFID etc to monitor the process.

Conclusion: Vanguards of Excellence

The rot in Nigeria is like a festering ulcer, ugly and painful. We have to move closer to government at all levels, and possess our possessions by forcing them to partner with us. The era of going cap in hand should gradually come to an end; and we should begin to work out a new vision of a country whose citizens are willing to build and not to destroy, ready to bring their creative ingenuity and resilience to re-moulding and remodeling the nation. Let CSOs take the lead in showing that they can do more with less, and that the little they access now is no excuse for mediocrity. Many people have all manners of prejudices against CSOs as profligate, hard currency earners, money minded, corrupt. Many of course know too that CSOs are a hope to the people. Let us be vanguards of excellence and be it in the remotest parts of Kano or in the metropolis of Abuja, anyone who encounters us should be transformed not just by the service rendered but by the love and care that defines that encounter. Our country needs a revolution. But it is 'a revolution of love', as Pope Benedict XVI said in in Africae Munus(no.26). This will be marked by the 'preferential attention…given to the poor, the hungry, the sick…to the stranger, the disadvantaged, the prisoner, the immigrant…(Ibid no.27). Everyone has a stake to foster this spirit of change.

References

'Special Event 25 September: Outcome Document', United Nations General Assembly 2013

Vatican Council ll The Concilliar and Post Concilliar Documents. Austin Flannery,O.P., ed.(Northport: Costello Publishing Company, 1975).

On the Development of Peoples(Populorum Progression). Encyclical Letter of His Holiness Pope Paul VI. (Nairobi: Paulines Publications Africa,1990)

Africa's Commitment(Africae Munus).Post-Synodal Apostolic Exhortation of His Holiness Pope Benedict XVI to the Bishops, Clergy, Consecrated Persons and the Lay Faithful on the Church in Africa in Service to Reconciliation, Justice and Peace.(Nairobi:Paulines Publications Africa,2011).

"Justice in the World".

Note 1. The idea of a Fund while being original, the framework is based on the research carried out by the International Center for Non Profit law in 2010

Note 2. A study of the Fund has been carried out in thirteen countries. The countries are Albania, Azerbaijan, Croatia, Hungary, Kazakhstan, Jordan, Poland, South Africa, Turkey, Estonia, Sweden, the United Arab Emirates and the United Kingdom.

CHAPTER ELEVEN

WHY CHURCHES ARE WRONG TARGETS OF WESTERN PROVOCATION OF MUSLIMS

One needs to know the psychology of the ordinary Muslim to understand his actions, even if one may not condone them. For the average Christian, the name of Jesus is holy, sacred, sacrosanct. It is even a commandment to keep holy the name of God and not misuse it, and as the Christian believes Jesus is God the Son, he loves that name, he adores that name, he worships that name; for it is a name invested with power and authority to heal and to bless. Ordinarily Jesus is not a name the Christian should use to curse others but these days we hear of people wishing others dead in the name of Jesus. A classic case was that which I heard about a young woman who was tired of a sick relative and brought a pastor to pray for her death; when the prayer was not successful after several days, she starved the sick woman to death. The source of this story claims to have been an eye witness. And when I asked why the police was not invited the answer I got was another question: 'Police ?', as if it was something so totally unthinkable and inappropriate in our clime. The name of Jesus is meant primarily to be a blessing although many have abused its usage.

I imagine that if someone said something scandalous or blasphemous about Jesus, the average Christian would feel offended. He might see this as a joke taken too far and warn the person for his own sake, so that God's punishment would not be visited upon him/her. He might then pray for the forgiveness of the person 'for he knoweth not what he is doing.' Movies have been made about Jesus that put him in blasphemous light. More than twenty five years ago, while training as a priest I watched one called The Last Temptation of Jesus. Jesus was portrayed in that movie as having left the cross and got married with children but if I can remember correctly, the producer was trying to project this blasphemy as an illusion in the mind of Jesus as he hung there on the cross, which Jesus promptly discarded and went ahead to give his life, as he realized that Satan had masked as an angel and seduced him to abandoning his mission of salvation. There have been other straight forward and outright blasphemies. Not to talk of books, the most recent and perhaps most famous being Dan Brown's 2003 *The Da Vinci Code*. A movie was even made out of it. I was serving in a parish in the US when this book was published, and I still remember the excitement of my pastor who finished his copy and asked me to borrow. I refused. I only read it a year later when it was buzzing everywhere. As a priest, when you read church history, you learn to not be scandalized, so I already had an attitude when I read Dan Brown's blasphemy.

Christian activists would usually advocate for books that are blasphemous to be banned or such movies to not be screened. The effect may then be that it elicits interest and many people want to buy or pay to watch. The West loves scandals. These Western societies have undergone historical transformations that have affected their cultural psyche, such as Enlightenment, which promulgated individualism and relativism among other ideas. In relativism especially the belief was fostered that all cultures and ideas have equal merit. The enlightenment also set the pace for accelerated scientific inquiry. It is not surprising therefore that although it has been stretched to its limit, the most important value in western society is perhaps the freedom of the individual. Freedom of expression in this context is seen as one of the most important fundamental human rights. The expectation would be that you either wrote a rejoinder or went to court if you felt your rights were abused.

On the other hand many Christians believe it is not their duty to defend God, as in to physically fight for God. They believe that God can fight for himself. They are brought up with the "turn the other cheek" admonition of the Lord Jesus.

Those who live with or relate with Muslims must know that they never joke at all with the name of the holy Prophet Mohammed. A Muslim is brought up to respect that name, to even ransom himself and 'his parents' for that name. A Christian may resist attempts that force him/her to deny the name of Jesus and may even allow himself to be killed and therefore become a martyr; but a Muslim would express righteous anger which may lead him to take his life and that of others if s/he feels the name of the holy Prophet has been blasphemed. This accounts for why when the name of the holy prophet is insulted anywhere in the world, especially in Western nations, there are demonstrations in parts of Africa as well, especially Nigeria, which could even turn violent. Fortunately the Charlie Hebdo provocation and the 2015 7th January shooting did not reverberate violently in Nigeria with any deaths. Unfortunately in Nigeria's neighbor, Niger Republic, a country not really known for religious violence, churches were torched and five persons each were killed in Niamey and Zinder, as about one thousand youths went on rampage as a reaction to the French publication. Perhaps the many deaths we have recorded in Nigeria as a result of religion based on the Boko Haram terrorism has put a measure of restrain, although recently, in 2016 a woman was killed in Kano because she was accused of blasphemy, and a Redeemed Pastor's wife itinerant preacher was killed early one morning in Abuja when she was preaching, although at the time of writing it was not clear who the assailants were.

We remember that in 2006 more than 16 deaths were recorded in Bornu and Katsina because of a cartoon by Kurt Westergaard in far away Denmark depicting the holy Prophet in bad light. Many hotels and shops were burnt.

The focus here is that if the intention is to express anger against Christians in West Africa for provocation that occurs in Western nations because they are supposedly Christian nations, the anger then is very well misplaced. The reason is that these nations are no longer Christian nations, they could be any other thing but Christian. In deed these nations may as well be Muslim nations as well. The reason is simple: citizens of European nations have gradually lost their heritage and become more or less free thinkers. Although there are new forecasts in terms of growth in church attendance because of migrants from Africa and Eastern European countries like Romania and Poland, as recently as 2013, church attendance in the UK was only 10% of the adult population; that is out of every 300,000 persons, only 15 persons were active members of any church (http//://www.theguardian.com/world/2014/jun/03/church-attendance-propped-immigrants-study). I once took charge of a parish in the UK, and on Sunday mornings the family next door would have their children playing in their garden. I used to imagine whether when these children grew up they would know anything about Christianity. I have attended church in many European capitals and all I found were a few old men and women and scores of migrants mostly from Asia and Africa. Europe is no more a Christian continent, it is a secular continent. Period. Statistics have shown rather an increase in the number of Muslims in European nations with Germany topping the list followed by France and the United Kingdom. With the low birth rate of Europeans and the higher birthrate of Arab migrants, it will be possible in a few decades that the practicing Muslim population in Europe would be higher than the practicing Christian population in Europe. It is therefore misplaced to transfer anger felt against European agnostics or free thinkers or pagans against West African Christians.

While we should strive for understanding among the religions, I must say that it is a few extremists who give the bad name to the Islamic religion. Islam may mean peace but these few extremists project Islam as anything but peaceful.

Most Muslims would feel angry at blasphemies directed against the holy Prophet but would not go to the extent of expressing this anger in violence. However everyone must do their best to change the narrative, beginning with an upbringing of children that sows seeds of respect for others' religion. Our children should be taught that not everyone can be a member of their religion, and that that does not make them inferior or superior, rather different. Our children should be taught that their religion is precious, and so is that of others; our children should be taught true sacrifice as being there for one another, and respecting the life God has given to them and others; our children should be taught that taking the life of another under any circumstances cannot be a work that pleases God.

CHAPTER TWELVE

STATE GOVERNORS AND ECONOMIC GROWTH

State governors occupy an extremely strategic position in the development of Nigeria. Imagine what would happen if we had men of vision and selfless service manning the affairs at the thirty six federating units. But alas, what is common is that very few go in with a clear idea of what to do. The enormous power and authority granted them by the constitution soon gets into their heads and they realize they are emperors. Other arms of government become mere appendages. And so in the real sense of it, at state level, there is only one arm of government, and this arm is one man, the governor.

Many a governor has used his position to enhance his personal economy, rather than build the economy of the state. When they embark on projects, apart from social infrastructures like roads, hospitals, water works, electricity distribution lines, many have little or no bearing on the economic growth of the state. Even the social infrastructure is awarded to companies with conflicts of interest, and the infrastructure becomes almost useless and needing renovation as soon as it is opened for business. A past time of some governors is to build giant retail shopping outlets or meeting venues in the name of growing the economy. These places then adorn the landscape. Donald Duke built Tinapa, a wasteful tourist moribund monument, while Liyel Imoke borrowed billions to build another white elephant called convention centre. Ondo State has also built an international conference centre with billions of state resources and perhaps a few other states have followed suit. Of course the idea is that high profile meetings would be held in these facilities and the state capitals would become a Geneva or Stockholm of sorts. And you ask, how many meetings would be held in a year that would reap the benefits of such often inflated expenditure ? How many jobs would these retail outlets create ? How much tourist traffic would this draw to the state ? The giant retail shopping centres would have made greater sense as complements to an industrial sector.

What grows the economy is the productive sector. The productive sector creates goods or services which can be traded locally and far away, and this in itself creates jobs and workers in turn spend to purchase other goods and services.   The ready local market and the 'exportable' nature of the products combined with adequate spending, then help to grow the economy. 'Exportability' here does not necessarily refer to international exports, although this is far better because of ability to earn foreign exchange. Rather this includes the fact that the goods and services are in demand in other parts of the country. I remember when an erstwhile military governor in Cross River State had the fantastic idea of establishing cottage industries in each local government area. Alas, they were left to rot because there was no follow up by successive governors. Donald Duke attempted to undertake the industrial approach with cashew nut factories, rice mills and so on but again that was abandoned. Liyel Imoke claims to have funded 141 community interest groups and to have disbursed 1.4 billion naira to 650 farmers and to have trained over 14,000 medium and small scale entrepreneurs. These figures are paltry compared to needs, and much more needs to be done.

Many governors may have done a lot in the provision of social infrastructure, which is an enabler; but current governors need to take firmer steps that would generate investment in the productive sector. I believe that it is time for every state government to domesticate what the federal government was doing under Jonathan with regard to the **You -Win** program. There should be many of our young men and women with bright ideas out there who can transform the productive sector and create jobs but have no access to capital. States should put resources together to fund these ideas which should grow small and medium scale enterprises, as our Central Bank and our commercial banks continue to work against the economy with high interest rates. The only clog is that many Nigerians regard what comes from government as largess and do not apply themselves to an accountable usage. But perhaps this new Buhari era might inspire some self-restraint beside linking up with credible NGOs to monitor these programs. State governments should study how Okonjo Iweala managed to overcome the corruption that should normally exist in such ventures and ensure that it does not become an avenue for awarding grants or soft loans to cronies who do not have the least business acumen.

More importantly, state governments should go in search of companies that manufacture the goods we use in Nigeria and invite them to come and establish here. Nigeria imports almost everything. No economy can grow that is overly dependent on imports, even of basic things. The globalization or liberalization of trade has made it such that Nigeria opens her doors to all kinds of products that are manufactured in- country and their comparative lower price value drives our own goods under, leading to the low capacity utilization of our industries. At some point, we have to realize that this kind of liberalism cannot grow our economy.

The so called foreign direct investment has been mostly in financial assets, paper money that does not add much value to the economy. Foreigners rush to buy our bonds and stocks because of our higher interest rates and pull out their funds as soon as there is the slightest economic tremor. This is not investment, where our books can show positive trillions today and negative trillions tomorrow. If foreigners have confidence in our economy, they will invest in real structures, equipment and machinery, they will invest in real productive enterprises. Very few governors actually have engaged in investment drives aside from the pleasure trips which they undertake with their cronies fully paid for by public funds. How come that with so many trips overseas there are no investments in the real sector of the economy ? Many years ago I kept wondering why our governments never attracted any solar-power assembly and or manufacturing companies to Nigeria, seeing the enormous potential market in Nigeria and the intractable problem of electricity. Years afterwards Nigeria became the destination of all kinds of poor quality solar batteries, inverters and solar panels from China and India. Even now there is an opportunity with the new research that solar panels could be manufactured with elements from salty sea waters.

Our politicians have not helped matters. They go on embezzling funds which they divert to the economies of other nations instead of finding ways to invest within the country, since we cannot stop the stealing anyway. Imagine what 6 billion US Dollars could do to the economy of Nigeria !

The point is that we need our governments at all levels to be more creative with enabling investments. Government still plays a crucial role in growing the economy no matter what the apologists of free trade tell us. I see many local farmers struggling to make ends meet when the local government could have supported them with seeds and agricultural extension services. I see many young men and women loitering around the villages when the local government could have supported them to own fish farms, poultries and other forms of animal husbandry with the entire value chain. I see communities growing because maybe an influential person has gone to bring an extractive company somewhere, and the state government cannot enable housing development !

It is good that President Muhammadu Buhari is bent on recovering stolen funds. What will be done with those funds ; dividing them among state governments for further division into security votes and sundry inexplicable expenditures ? Could these funds be kept aside for funding creative ideas in the real sector of the economy ? Can Nigeria spark an industrial revolution through the creativity of her teeming youths who often excel out of the shores of this nation which has often threatened to stunt and devastate their future ?

CHAPTER THIRTEEN

AS CENTRAL BANK BECOMES BUREAU DE CHANGE

Finally the Nigerian government capitulated to the economists. Rather than a fixed exchange rate, the naira is being thrown to market forces which determine its 'true' value. Already it is being reported that consistently for a number of days, at the parallel market, the naira stood at 350 to the dollar, going up to 400 to the dollar at some point. As we capitulate, we know that this is not the true value of the naira but a forced value, forced by low foreign exchange earnings, insider trading and round tripping and a panicky greedy elite which obsessively stockpiles the dollar.

I still sincerely believe that the naira is undervalued. Take a hair cut for instance. Where in the United States would you get a haircut for one dollar ? Haircuts are done for twenty dollars whereas you could get your hair cut for two hundred naira, which is not even up to a dollar, based on the floating rate. Or where could you get a meal at one dollar ? Yet you could get *mama put* at two hundred naira or less. Where could you have a taxi drop at two dollars ? Yet you could have a drop at three hundred naira. The purchasing power parity of the naira versus the dollar clearly shows that the naira is undervalued.

For a while it made sense to peg the exchange rate. Central Bank of Nigeria did all within its power to save the naira. All the measures it took would have been successful in some other country, but there is a factor exclusive to us as a people, the

Nigerian factor, which would frustrate the best ideas of the common good and poison them with egotistic desires. The fixed exchange was becoming too lucrative for those with official access to forex; civil servants on foreign trips, government officials on overseas medical treatment, influential citizens with children schooling abroad; bankers also had a field day as it was reported that behind the counter, they negotiated with importers who needed forex, made them sign off on the official rate, and collected the difference under the counter. Ultimately the nation was losing while a few individuals were getting rich. The wide gulf between the official and parallel market rates made it such that only a saint already living in heaven would not be tempted to devise means of taking advantage of the system. Therefore as the Monetary Policy Committee has decided to adopt a flexible exchange rate policy, it is perhaps better, not because the market rate is the real value of the naira but to eliminate the temptation and the corruption.

It is good that government overcame the temptation to retain a fixed exchange rate for critical sectors of the economy, because it truly needed to convince Nigerians what those sectors were. For instance how were we sure that we wouldn't recede to the Abacha days where whatever the Head of State needed at the time became critical, such that while others got forex at the higher official rate, favoured cronies were using fewer naira to buy forex, selling it off at the higher official rate and using the excess naira to buy more forex, in an endless opportunity cycle ? What guarantees would a government which had made anticorruption its main agenda of governance given, that there wouldn't be a repeat of such abuse of access? Even with the outgoing wide gulf between the official rate and the parallel market rate, there was an accusation leveled against a presidential aide of having made hundreds of millions of naira from the parallel market. Well, only a fool would go to the bank to change his forex at official rate when he or she has access to a legitimate platform that could give him more. Perhaps, to eliminate this hypocrisy, this double standard, the flexible exchange rate is welcome.

But the new policy must be something that really benefits Nigerians. In my understanding, formerly individuals in the CBN and the deposit money banks yanked off the profits; now government, through the CBN has become a mega bureau de change. It means that rather than give the hard earned dollars away to bank officials and their collaborators at ridiculous rates for them to devise means of smiling to their *soak-aways* (no more smiling to the bank since they now hide the money in soak-away pits), the CBN would sell forex to banks a little below the prevailing market rate. In practical terms, in April 2016 CBN sold 669 million dollars to deposit money banks. Assuming it sold this at 198 naira to the dollar, it made only one naira atop the 197 window, and if the banks were to be faithful to sell this at 200 naira per dollar, would collectively make one billion three hundred and thirty eight million naira, although it is doubtful that this was the case. Or even if they were saintly enough to do so, those who got these monies wouldn't be; they would find ways to perform miracles with it. So now my understanding of a flexible exchange rate would be that, taking the figure of April, from 669 million dollars, instead of making a paltry 669 million naira selling to banks, the CBN would make something like two hundred billion, seven hundred million naira(N200,700,000,000) if it sold the dollar at 300 naira each or somewhat less if they sold at 285. With this amount of money coming in every month, we hope that government officials would not go junketing but would apply the funds to economic development, which should always mean the development of peoples.

Perhaps this is a manifestation of the truism that every disappointment is a blessing. Government should see forex trading as a business with huge profits and make as much money as it could from the business. The other worry would be putting the money into good use. Though I have not made a study of it, but it seems that when special agencies are established, they accelerate infrastructural development faster. Petroleum Trust Fund(PTF) did far more than the government was doing. I still remember that it did the road to my village in addition to the water-works. Contractors had more confidence in SURE-P because payment for work was guaranteed. Perhaps whatever CBN makes from this flexible exchange business should be put into a Special Infrastructure Fund and a board created to manage it. A special focus could be developing access infrastructure to tourism sites. How is the road to Mambilla Plateau or Yankari Game Reserve ? Why can't there be a fast train to Obudu Cattle Ranch ? Or a good road to the Oban Corridor of the Cross River National Park ? How can we mouth diversifying the economy and not be strategic in providing access infrastructure ? Leaving the money as part of ministries would just be business as usual, and before long, the civil servants would show politicians the ways and means of siphoning all the money with nothing to show except poor roads constructed by usually corruptible Chinese companies and fifth rate imports from China. What systems are we putting in place to ensure that while Buhari is fighting corrupt past politicians, the corruption right under his nose doesn't become the mother of all corruptions. Let this government tell Nigerians what it would do differently with this flexible exchange bonanza.

CHAPTER FOURTEEN

BUHARI AND THE PRIDE OF THE BLACKMAN

At first the expectations concerning the Buhari government were almost messianic in nature. Nigerians wanted so much change, so very fast that any excuse to the contrary would have been seen as an un-readiness on the part of the new government to plunge headlong into executing a mantra which had catapulted them into power, change. The challenges remain quite enormous and the time and resources needed to combat them so short in their supply that as quick as they are to trust, many Nigerians have been quick to dismiss the regime as a failure. I hope and pray that Nigerians would be patient and faithful and fight the pessimism that may have enveloped them.

While Muhammadu Buhari is not a Messiah, the situation reminds one of ancient Jewish expectations. They longed and prayed for a Messiah but when he came, they did not recognize him, because he wasn't the messiah of their mold. The Jews expected someone divinely instrumented to wage war with the colonial forces of occupation, someone who would dislodge the tyranny and re-establish the Davidic Kingdom. For centuries they prayed and hoped; then Jesus the Christ came, the incarnate Son of God, born of the Virgin Mary, into the family of Joseph the carpenter. According to some commentators, the Greek word used for carpenter actually could be translated as 'job-man', that kind of general purpose workman you could call to fix anything. Jesus the Christ born into very humble background even though of the

Davidic lineage, didn't really fit into their mental image. And in spite of the ferocity of his message, his fearlessness and his personal authority, he went about performing miracles that had no bearing at all to the political expectations. He healed the sick, cured the leprous, cast out demons, cured the blind and raised the dead. And when he fed the five thousand, something akin to what a politician would do and they wanted to force him to become king, he made away from them. Even John the Baptist was forced to send emissaries to Jesus the Christ to ask if he were the one to come or they were to wait for another. At the end he was arrested on trumped up charges and sentenced to death on the cross. And while it became a stumbling block for the Jews and a thing of folly to the more philosophical Greeks, the death of the Christ on the Cross and his subsequent resurrection, became for all humanity a means of salvation. While he was viewed from an enclavist, regionalist and temporal prism, he offered rather what was cosmic and eternal.

One of the places I pass time whenever I visit Rome is the Termini Station. It is Rome Central Train station, and there is a wonderful bookshop you could get the latest books in major European languages. I stumbled on a book by Francis Fukuyama the political scientist, entitled, *Political Order and Political Decay*. As I scanned through the content, I took keen interest because there was a chapter on Nigeria. I settled down to read it. I went away very sad, because all he had to say was the truth about my beloved nation, the truth of its culture and nature, the truth of its corruption. Let me quote from a passage in the book : "Nigeria's real institutional deficit lies in the first two categories: lack of strong modern and capable state and absence of rule of law that provides property rights, citizens security, and transparency in transactions. These two deficits are related. Rather than having a modern state that can provide necessary public goods like roads, ports, schools, and public health on an impersonal basis, the Nigerian government main activities is predatory or…prebendal: it is engaged in extraction of rent and their distribution to other members of political elites. This leads to the routine violation of the rule of law…" (Fukuyama, 2014).

He argued that not only was the Nigerian State weak and without technical capacity, it had gross moral deficit which prevents it from clobbering a nation together. "Why is it that the Nigerian state and rule of law ended up being so extraordinarily weak ?", Fukuyama wondered, and went on in the next chapter to examine arguments concerning geography and climate which position certain nations as culturally and politically disposed to building strong institutions and a strong state, and others with a propensity towards producing weak institutions and therefore a weak state, effectively reviving and reviewing the argument on whether geography hinders or contributes to national development. Anyway that might be the subject of another day but for me the book changed my perspective on my expectations concerning the administration of Muhammadu Buhari, President and Commander in Chief of the Nigerian Armed Forces.

The task before Buhari is not an infrastructural one, at least not physical infrastructure. Thank God oil prices are down and there isn't as much money as there used to be and so waste and naked stealing of public funds would be drastically reduced. I for one believe that less than fifty percent of accrued funds were actually ploughed into governance, so the drop in the price of oil levels off to the level of actual expenditure for governance, so there really is no deficit except in bloated figures in the normally cosmetic budget. The only danger is that most governors may steal all that is left over and nothing would remain at all for governance. Otherwise I would pray that the situation remain as it is until a culture of prudence and service was firmly established. Which brings me to my perception of the Buhari presidency.

We seem to forget often that there are other tiers of government, or at least another tier of government, since the state governors have refused to allow the local governments function practically as another tier even if it were not theoretically so; and so we have tended to focus more on the presidency, leaving our governors to remain the most unhindered thieves in our history as a nation; expectedly we have focused on Muhammadu Buhari as if Nigeria is a unitary and not a federal government.

The task before Buhari is an ethical one. Ethics is usually based on morality, and thank God Nigeria is mostly of two religious traditions that subscribe to a similar moral code; even our African traditional religion never encourages anyone to murder, steal or take over one's wife and property or dishonor one's parents. While morality may be a set of broad principles concerning right and wrong, ethical principles might be a more detailed code of principles or values influencing behavior. There is such a big gap between our moral principles and our current values, such that I once heard a young man say 'If I am elected into office I will scrape away even the very paint on the walls...' Over the decades we have totally corrupted the sense of the common good among our people, we have bastardised nationhood and the sacrifice of service and presented Nigeria to present and future generations as worse than a state of nature where survival is not even about the fittest but for the most corrupt; and where access to wealth is not hard work and talent but access to the public till.

How can the ordinary citizen regain trust in government ? How does s/he get convinced that government could make an objective needs assessment and site projects or programs based on such objective criteria and not because it is the paternal or maternal home of the governor or his close associates ? The Speaker of the House of Representatives informed us in an audience in the midst of the budget padding scandal, that if you were not a director in the federal ministry, there was no way a project could be located in your constituency; that the budget proposal as was presented to the House had no single project located in his own constituency, and so he had to use his office to allocate projects in his own constituency! How do we start doing things on a need and human rights basis ? How do we come to the sense that a public servant who steals Nigeria's money at the headquarters should not be celebrated back home ? How do we regain the sense that our politics should be with principles and that Nigeria's money is common wealth ? How do we trust that our children could go to our public universities and graduate successfully without having to bribe their way ? How do we trust that the policeman would not twist our case just because of a higher bidder ? How do we give confidence to our law enforcement agencies such that they are bigger than the individuals who are presently 'bigger' than the institutions and therefore above the law ? How do we ensure consistency such that court judgments are not rubber stamps of powerful individuals ? How do we make the average Nigerian want to die to save the nation rather than preferring a whole nation to perish while s/he flourishes ?

These for me, are agenda for Buhari. Anyone can build a road or a dam. But not everyone can change a mindset and a culture. I hear Buhari once returned from the UK on Premium Economy. That action alone could save money to build a bridge across a river; because if the head could so do, why would his subordinates do otherwise ? I recently saw government officials flying first class on my way from London and I asked myself, why would anyone fly first class on public funds ? I take it for granted that he would put his ministers under check. The concern is with governors. Irrespective of what the constitution says, the president has some leverage with governors. Buhari must really rescue the ordinary Nigerian from these emperors called governors, many of who are really a gang of macro thieves and plunderers. He should begin with those of his party and not exclude others. He should not single out only those that criticize him, the way Fayose's case is being perceived. A frequent chat with governors based on security reports should go a long way to put them on track. Immunity does not preclude investigation; Fawehinmi had obtained a judgment from the supreme court that a public official with immunity could be investigated even if not prosecuted. Let Vice President Osinbanjo build the roads and the bridges and the dams. Let Buhari rebuild our bastardized psyche and culture and trust and restore the pride of the Black man which this nation has been so proficient in doing worldwide damage.

CHAPTER FIFTEEN

50 LIVES WORTH A BULLET

Some years ago I was in Israel when I watched a news footage about a gun wielding Israeli soldier who was attacked by some Palestinian youths and all he did was unsuccessfully use the gun to fend off the stones that were hurled at him. Next day I heard in the news that the soldier had been court martialed for failing to defend himself even when he had his weapon. I believe that ever since, Israeli soldiers have shown no hesitation in using their guns in self-defense when attacked by Palestinians with stones.

By their training, especially in the Nigerian military, there is nothing a military man or woman hates as being impeded in his/her duties or actions by 'bloody' civilians. The least soldier is trained to hold in high contempt any civilian except one of a high rank put ceremonially in their charge, for example a minister of defense. Soldiers are trained with such pent up emotion as always to desire action, and it is now clear that all those stories about our troops running away from the battle front were either because they had no weapons, for a soldier is his weapon, or such actions were led by Boko Haram sympathisers.

When I read the story of the confrontation between the men of the Nigerian army and El Zakzakay's Shi'ites my first concern was to find out the religion of the Chief of Army Staff. I was greatly relieved to affirm that he is Muslim; for I know that if Buratai were Christian the story would have taken a totally different turn. Our military have done their best to remain professional but many

Nigerians would find it extremely difficult to justify Muslims of any sect being killed because of a Christian, even if that Christian were commander in chief.

I read a newspaper article The Duke Would Have Turned, where the writer opined that in other climes, the chief of army staff convoy would have taken a different route but that in Nigeria, the army must have its way even if that leaves scores of people dead. He then made suggestions on other penalties that could have been applied to the Shiites by the local government. Of course these alternatives are laughable, for as revealed, these Shiites live above the law and have no respect for any constituted authority. They go to wherever they please on foot in a disorderly procession and occupy both lanes; you just had to make way for them. Organized processions take the right lane and leave the other for traffic but these adherents have no room for others. It is useless taking them to court because they would not obey, and the police would be powerless before them. Sheikh Gumi said they reigned supreme in Zaria for forty years.

Wherever these groups exist, they show the weakness and the incapacity of the state. In modern state theory, the state should have the monopoly of violence, but these groups usually portray the underbelly of the Nigerian state as weak, rotten and replete with noxious matter. State officials would bow and tremble before these simpletons, because of their capacity to wield violence. Besides most Nigerians have respect for what is religious, and this respect overshadows respect for the rule of law. Only the military could have insisted on having passage, as they did, and at the cost of several human lives ! Videos show how soldiers canvassed a safe passage for their general and how the Shiite adherents refused to make way and became violent. I am very certain that from the onset there was restraining order given to the soldiers by Buratai; for the ordinary impulse of the rank and file is to jump in and disperse the crowd with *koboko*, which would have made it a dangerous mission, with the adherents holding knives and stones and sticks. They would have beaten the soldiers blue, and perhaps killed a few, in which case the soldiers would go away and return to level the entire space, including any living thing seen around the perimeter. It seems to me then that there was an actual threat which occasioned the shootout, especially as these adherents neither value their lives nor that of others.

Nevertheless I lament the downward spiral in the value of life that is so common in our country Nigeria. The level of indoctrination is so high that for religious reasons, an adherent holds very cheaply such a precious gift as the gift of life. Religious adherents are taught from childhood to sacrifice for God and to see their faith as superior to their lives. This is why we have martyrs in Christianity as well. How I wished every religion respected life as a fundamental gift and right, so that even if one had to allow a life to be taken for religious reasons, it would be one's own life and not others'. Leaders of religions the world over should take it as a paramount crusade to institute respect for human rights especially the fundamental right to life as criteria for the authenticity of religious practice.

The recent happenings in the United States concerning police brutality and cover up show that being trigger happy is not the preserve of Nigerian police or soldiers. But there must be a way in which gunning down a human being would not be as easy as hunting down a sport. If we hunt down a deer we could make a bonfire and have a barbecue. What would we do with human carcass, than to dig a grave and bury it, a human being whom you once could argue with, laugh, eat, pray and work with ? Could there be a way our armed forces would reserve live bullets for the real enemy and use only bullets that may immobilize but not kill, for the civilian population? That way notorious but not-fatally armed persons could be immobilized, arrested and prosecuted. Imagine if the army had used these kinds of bullets on the Shiites!

Those of us that are enlightened get very concerned about the audacity of some of the adherents of these religious sects. For instance I find the average Muslim so friendly, dependable and law abiding. Perhaps it is a product of history and we can't blame our Muslim brothers who can't really do something about these violent sects. We know that Muslims are mostly divided into Sunnis and Shiites, based on the controversy surrounding the legitimate successor to Prophet Muhammed, with the Sunnis holding that it was right for Abu Bakr who wasn't a blood relative of the Prophet to be chosen as successor, and the Shiites holding that it should be the holy Prophet's cousin, Ali. Shiites make up only about 10 to 15% of the Muslim population in the world. Nevertheless Shiites and Sunnis both hold dear the fundamentals of the Islamic faith, differing mainly in the emphasis they place on certain aspects such as the role of the Imam, and the 'Ashura', the Shiite memorial ritual of Hussein, Ali's younger son who was martyred, an event they mark every year with all kinds of rituals. We know that intra-differences and prejudices could be as strong, if not stronger than differences *ad extra*. But I think it is time for everyone, Muslim or Christian to take up his/her holy books and read them and understand them and seek for guidance from those who may be wiser, so that we end the hero worship and the consequent toll on God's gift of life which value is compared now only to our sliding Naira currency. If it isn't a death toll from Boko Haram, it is civilian military confrontation or accidents at pipeline vandalizing sites or collateral damage arising from military expeditions. Add recently victims of gas explosion disasters. Behind these figures were once concrete living human beings with hopes and aspirations. It is sad.

CHAPTER SIXTEEN

SUPPORTING NIGERIA TO MEET THE 20% UNCONDITIONAL CARBON EMISSION REDUCTION TARGETS *An address given by the Executive Secretary/CEO of Caritas Nigeria and JDPC Fr. Evaristus Bassey on the Occasion of a Courtesy Visit to the Honourable Minister of Environment on 8th July 2016*

Honourable Minister, Caritas Nigeria and JDPC are agencies of the Catholic Bishops Conference of Nigeria(CBCN). They are established to be an outreach of the Bishops as far as humanitarian and human development issues are concerned, and accommodate members of all faiths or no faiths as beneficiaries.

Laudato Si and Carbon Neutrality: Ever since Pope Francis came out with the landmark encyclical on the environment called *Laudato Si*, Caritas Nigeria and JDPC have organized sensitization campaigns, with the Bishops of Nigeria advising many church institutions to work towards being carbon neutral, especially by installing renewable energy sources for their power needs and promoting ecological conversion, as directed by Pope Francis. Our Catholic Secretariat of Nigeria for instance has cut down on its fossil fuel consumption drastically, by installing solar panels, similarly our vehicles are using extreme fuel treatments (XFTs) that help in carbon emission reductions. These are small steps which hopefully should contribute towards mitigating the impact of climate change.

Strengthening Regulatory Bodies: We want to commend Mr. President's commitment towards the Ogoni clean up. However we want to advise that the regulatory agencies be strengthened and always on the alert so that we don't have situations where we only react to issues. For instance NESREA should be strengthened so that it is far reaching in its capacity to ensure professionalism and corruption free Environmental Impact Assessments (EIAs). Corruption is not only when money is stolen, but when processes are skewed to achieve aims that are against the public interest or when regulations are overlooked. The Extended Product Stewardship Program which has as part of its package a product Buy Back program has it that notwithstanding the original brand owner, industrialists and importers are to 'establish a process for the collection, handling, transportation and final treatment of post-consumer products…" This extended stewardship program could help rid our country of much waste.

Permit us to observe that in this critical time of our age, where our actions could either lead to saving or destroying the Earth, our common home, as Environment Minister, you owe it to humanity to monitor very closely all projects that have potential to weigh in further ecological imbalance and damage no matter who is involved.

Collaborating to Meet Nigeria's 20% Emission Reduction: Caritas Nigeria and JDPC humbly request the Hon. Minister to use the strategy of deploying energy saving cook-stoves as a principal way of meeting the 20% unconditional target. There are technologists designing various stoves, which could be promoted through the clean development mechanism(CDM) for carbon credit. But presently the ***Save80*** Cookstove promoted by Yahaya Mohammed of DARE has already gone through the process and Nigeria could get back whatever she invests in this programme through the carbon credit.

If your ministry could plan for the deployment of about 2,592 Million Save80 stoves in 5 years for instance, this could target 20% of Households using biomass in Nigeria for cooking. **Economic Benefits:** Although this could cost about 37 million Euros, yet Nigeria could get back these funds from the 100 billion USD climate adaptation fund that is available during this period. It is estimated that up to 663 million Euros could accrue to Nigeria through carbon credit by 2020 and nearly 2 billion Euros by 2030. It therefore makes economic sense to undertake this endeavor.

Ecological Benefits: Our experts and partners have estimated that :

- CO_2 emission savings: - 9,070,000 metric tonnes p.a.
- Estimated CO_2 emissions savings by 2030: 136 Million metric tonnes p.a.
- Estimated 3,11Million matured trees saved annually.
- Estimated 46, 65 Million matured trees saved by 2030.
- Estimated annual sequestration of CO_2: 68,420 metric tonnes.
- Estimated sequestration of CO_2 by 2030: 1,026 miillion metric tonnes.
- Estimated reduction of deaths due to IAP: 6,000 p.a.
- Estimated reduction of deaths due to IAP: 90,000 by 2030.
- Estimated savings in Fuelwood procurement: 1,200 Naira/Month/Household.
- Estimated monthly savings in Fuelwood procurement by target households: 3, 1 billion Naira.
- Estimated annual savings in Fuelwood procurement by target households: 37, 3 Billion Naira.
- Estimated 1.5 billion naira savings on avoided tree felling p.a.(@ 500 Naira/matured tree).

Employment Benefits: Deploying the Save80 Cook-stoves would also assist in job creation, as many youths could learn how to assemble the stoves.

Health Benefits: The health of women and children who suffer from inhaled air pollution effects would also be minimized.

Request for Abandoned Stoves: Caritas Nigeria intends to deploy Save80 Stoves in 19 communities of the Oban corridor of the Cross River National Park. Although the magic boxes maybe bad by now, we request the Hon. Minister to allow access to Caritas Nigeria to distribute the stoves abandoned at the National Park Headquarters.

Conclusion: Caritas Nigeria and JDPC are platforms the Bishops have established to reach out to the poor. As this is a government of change, we are ready to collaborate with your ministry to ensure that 'no one is left behind especially those farthest from behind.' Thank you.

CHAPTER SEVENTEEN

ESTABLISHMENT OF GRAZING RESERVES IN NIGERIA: A PASTORAL REFLECTION BASED ON POPE FRANCIS' ENCYCLICAL LETTER LAUDATO SI

Introduction

In the light of current discussions surrounding the issue of grazing reserves for nomadic Fulani herdsmen in Nigeria, it has become necessary to offer some pastoral reflection, hoping that some guidance could be given that may facilitate a win-win situation.

Grazing reserves refer to tracts of land set aside by state authorities for use by farmers and pastoralists for the feeding of cattle and sheep and other economic animals. In a context of poor access to land by majority of citizens of Nigeria, with a population that is up to 70% dependent on subsistent agriculture coupled with the challenge presented by climate change, this issue needs to be critically reviewed and a cost benefit analysis made, not only in terms of business or economic terms but social and environmental perspectives as well.

In Nigeria, the first attempt to legislate on grazing reserves goes back to 1964 with the Grazing Reserve Act. The double intention was to restrict the ever increasing encroachment on grazing areas by food crop farmers and to attempt to sedenterize nomadic Fulani. Many of the proposed reserves were forest areas already reserved by government and when eventually some were not gazetted as grazing reserves they could not be protected from encroachment by populations who faced an increasing need for land for crop production and subsistence. The herdsmen that settled around the grazing reserves were mainly those already known to have settled in the surrounding areas. The act did not therefore succeed in sedenterizing the nomadic Fulani, especially with the challenge of low yield of grasses in the semi-arid parts of the North where many of these reserves were located. The over-grazing on these tracts of land sometimes often led to bare earth and feed insecurity for cattle and forced livestock that were in these reserved grazing areas to be moved for better pasture because of the unhealthy condition of the livestock.

The age old practice of moving cattle down south during the dry season has continued unabated by the nomadic Fulani. Many communities in the South West, South East, South South, have historically been accustomed to seeing herdsmen drive their cattle seasonally through swaths of land in the outskirts of communities, with increasing sedentarization of some who migrate and settle in deep forests of many communities sometimes without community members being aware of their presence.

Current Demand for Grazing Reserves

Over the last two decades there has been an increase in the number of herdsmen heading south in pursuit of green pastures. With the continuous shrinking of the Lake Chad Basin there has been an influx of nomadic Fulani from neighbouring countries into Nigeria. Unlike previous decades where settlement was temporary, there have been an increase in number of herdsmen who settle permanently in communities, taking possession of yet to be used lands in those communities. Nomadic Fulani have tended to seek out the settlements of the more sedentary Fulani and in the course of mixing up with them may not have imbibed the culture of delineating between wild greenery or farm crop residues and cultivated farmland. While most herdsmen are said to respect public farms or agricultural estates, the incidence of cattle grazing on crops planted by subsistent farmers has been on the increase, fueling clashes with host communities. Having measured greater prevalence in northern states, hostilities between herdsmen and host communities have peaked in recent times in the South East. The intensity of these conflicts has caused many a Nigerian to speculate on a hidden agenda pursued by herdsmen.

A critical look at this migratory trend towards the south shows that it is not unconnected with the ecological conditions in the north of Nigeria. As early as the late 1980s reports have had it that even during a time of rain, maximum grass productivity in some of the reserves in the semi-humid regions "is very low(2250 kg/ha)" besides the poor nutritional value of the type of grass that grows in the region.[1] Presently up to 15 states in the north are being affected by the incidence of desertification; and in an article published in the Journal of Ecology and Natural Environment, Olagunju refers to relevant authorities that "over-grazing removes the vegetation cover that protects soil from erosion(UNCCD) and degrades natural vegetation that leads to desertification and decrease in the quality of rangelands(Sheikh and Soomro,2006)."

These ecological conditions have been made worse by the effect of climate change, leading to biodiversity loss among other hazards. Pope Francis observed that climate change "is a global problem with grave implications: environmental, social, economic, political and for the distribution of goods."[2]. For pastoralists, such "changes in climate to which animals and plants cannot adapt, lead them to migrate."[3] The effect of climate change on desertification has meant the loss of more cultivatable land and water sources. The poor use of ecological funds by government agencies too has meant that proactive measures to respond to the unfolding menace have not been wholeheartedly pursued, leaving not only a fodder and water crisis for livestock but food security crises for human populations in Nigeria as well.

Grazing Reserves and Nigerian Society

Ordinarily all parts of Nigeria consume meat from cattle and sheep. Access to markets for this protein source should mean the close proximity of livestock. This perhaps informs the allocation of territories to Cattle dealers who are mostly Hausa-Fulani in many cities in the South of Nigeria. The quest for grazing lands or ranches would mean that lands traditionally owned by ancestors of certain communities would be taken from them and assigned as reserves for livestock mostly owned or managed by herdsmen. Historically, whenever a grazing reserve was established in Nigeria, sedentary Fulani who moved in to occupy the reserves tended to see the land as 'Fulani land', being the principal tribe engaged in cattle rearing.[4] In spite of the ecological challenges aggravated by climate change and the obvious need for feed security for cattle, there is a growing perception in Nigeria especially among those in the South that any attempt to allocate land as grazing reserves from their ancestral lands would be a veiled effort to carve out enclaves for Fulani in areas where they have not been historically known to inhabit; many thus argue that such reserves, if at all, should be limited to northern regions, against the backdrop of recent clashes in the South East between herdsmen and host communities and against the background of Boko Haram terrorism.

One could argue that based on the national need for protein from cattle and the fact that the herdsmen are Nigerians, consideration should be made for grazing reserves or ranches in more fertile parts of Nigeria be it in the South South or South West, thereby ensuring that while ecological issues are being redressed, there is food security for the populace; the porous nature of our borders which makes it possible for non-Nigerian herdsmen to move easily into the country from neighbouring countries, makes it difficult to sustain this argument among sensitive populations who are not really certain of the motive of these foreigners who sometimes have a merciless passion for taking human life. Besides, grazing reserves may be useful for a few years until they suffer the effect of over-grazing which would bring about another vicious circle of demand for more reserves. The argument for grazing lands with all its economic benefits and yet its potential for ecology and conflict weighs therefore towards a more fundamental threat to human life and peaceful society. Many have argued that the intention to create more reserves is akin to creating a bigger problem by solving a problem. Pope Francis has advised in Laudato Si that "in the face of possible risks to the environment which may affect the common good now and in the future, decisions must be made "based on a comparison of the risks and benefits foreseen for the various possible alternatives"[5]. A more critical look at the matter of grazing reserves, balancing all environmental, economic, political and social angles is therefore necessary.

Considering Alternatives

The matter of grazing is as old as human culture itself. Abraham, patriarch of the Judeo-Christian and Islamic religions, had so many cattle and sheep, as well as his brother Lot, and the grazing fields could not sustain them both. Scripture says "the land was not able to support them, that they might dwell together, for their possessions were so great that they could not dwell together."[6] While there may be potential conflicts in handling grazing matters, sincerity of purpose and an uncompromising desire for peace as Abraham had, are fundamental to any intended solution. The charged atmosphere wherever herdsmen mix up with native communities down south suggests a dearth of this uncompromising desire for peace.

The participation of communities that would be potentially affected by any decision is very important from the onset. A top down approach where decisions are taken and those affected are informed and cajoled to buy in is to be avoided in the interest of good society. Whereas in the modern economy land becomes a question of title deed, manifested in the right of occupancy (R of O) or certificate of occupancy (C of O) , most rural communities in Nigeria still rely on ancestry for legitimacy and may not possess any title deeds. Government must therefore avoid an arrogance which tends to construct government as an omnipotent authority or beyond the sovereignty of the people. If possible community people should be trained in livestock rearing and given the option of establishing ranches within their communities which others may also make use of. A recent report had it that one of the causes of clashes are grazing fees herdsmen pay to community leaders, which then give them a sense of entitlement. Community leaders should endeavor to be transparent and carry community members along in such negotiations. If possible such fees should be avoided.

The insistence on grazing reserves should not be short sighted but consider how once forested areas would be turned into barren lands in the future. As Pope Francis said in Laudato Si, "the loss of forests and woodlands entails the loss of species which may constitute extremely important resources in the future, not only for food but also for curing disease and other uses."[7]

The Ministry of Agriculture should borrow a leaf from Israel, where arid desert lands have been turned into cultivable fields through green houses and innovative irrigation. In Mexico, a Jesuit University has developed capacity to nurse 12 million trees in green houses. These are innovative approaches which our governments need to pursue with much vigour and combat the desertification that is increasingly threatening crop viability on lands in the northern part of Nigeria. Luckily the Honourable Minister of Environment, Amina Mohammed is bent on pursuing a tough agenda against desert encroachment, as she pointed out recently during a visit to her office.

Pope Emeritus Benedict XVI had observed that "The external deserts in the world are growing, because the internal deserts have become so vast."[8] When man decenters himself from values which make him authentic to his faith, there is internal desertification. Corruption which has eaten deep into the fabric of the Nigerian society and has thrown up a culture of carelessness and mediocrity which has affected our approach to serious environmental issues is one of the factors of internal desertification with grave external consequences. Dealing with the corruption cankerworm and properly using ecological funds may bring about the necessary innovations that could turn around vast arid lands into productive ones.

Commercial cultivation of hay may be an approach that could be adopted if these arid lands are reclaimed through innovative processes. Better still the Federal Ministry of Industry, Trade and Investment could create the enabling environment for commercial ventures into fodder production by industrialists.

Conclusion

A concern for grazing reserves should not take the minds of authorities off resolving conflicts between herdsmen and farming communities. Going by reports from media houses, the acquisition of locally made arms by farming communities in readiness for defenses against attacks by Fulani herdsmen may only make future clashes more devastating, as herdsmen may be more ferocious in their attacks , and being better trained, with greater access to modern weaponry.

It still goes back to government therefore to strengthen the institutions of law enforcement. It is a weak state that allows its monopoly of the instruments of violence to be usurped by powerful individuals or groups. Where the citizenry lose hope and confidence in the ability of the state to guarantee protection of life and property, those who govern the state should question their performance of the core duty of state. The peaceful coexistence of populations in Nigeria no matter their economic and social standing should be a paramount task of government at all levels. We hereby paraphrase the words of Pope Francis in Laudato Si that any solution which we claim to offer to resolve issues will be powerless if as a people and a nation we lose our compass, and "lose sight of the great motivations which make it possible for us to live in harmony, to make sacrifices and to treat others well."[9].

While Christians in various communities should not allow themselves to be slaughtered like sheep, taking laws into their hands, and engaging in anti-Christian actions such as vengeance killings will not resolve any issues either. Even in these trying times, all men and women of goodwill are urged to live out the injunction from the Lord Jesus himself : " But I tell you, love your enemies and pray for those who persecute you." (Matthew 5:44).

References

1. S.A. Ingawa, G.Tarawali, R.von Kaufmann, Grazing Reserves in Sub-humid Nigeria, ILCA , Addis Ababa, 1989 Network paper no.22
2. Pope Francis, Laudato Si . Rome: Vatican Press, 2015. no.25
3. Ibid, no.25
4. Ingawa et al par. 22
5. Pope Francis, Laudato Si, no. 184
6. Genesis 13:6
7. Pope Francis, Laudato Si, no. 32
8. Benedict XVl, Homily for the Solemn Inauguration of the Petrine Ministry(24 april 2005):AAS 97 (2005) 710

Pope Francis, Laudato Si, no.200

CHAPTER EIGHTEEN

INDEGENISING SOLIDARITY: THE CASE OF CARITAS NIGERIA

By Evaristus Bassey

With dwindling world financial resources occasioned by the economic down turn, it is increasingly becoming more sensible to tap into the reservoir of goodwill that is available among our 30 million Catholics, and raise liquid resources for the financing of the social ministry of the church. The Nigerian church has marked more than a centenary and is ripe enough to spearhead what the Holy Father calls the 'globalization of solidarity' in the Post-Synodal Apostolic Exhortation Africae Munus[1].

In the same document the Holy Father says:

'Africa is capable of providing every individual and every nation of the continent with the basic conditions which will enable them to share in development. Africans will thus be able to place their God-given talents and riches at the service of their land and their brothers and sisters.'[2].

Basic conditions here may mean good governance, an independent judiciary, respect for human rights, and all the ingredients that make up modern democracy. For me, it is more or less a call to solidarity; for in this sense, it is becomes a recognition of the humanity and the dignity of the other, and committing to doing all that is within one's means to make it practically fruitful. The Catholic Bishops Conference of Nigeria(CBCN) therefore have provided a platform through Caritas Nigeria for the materialization of this call to solidarity.

In the 70s, with Murtala Muhammed and later Olusegun Obasanjo as military Head of State, there was the indigenization decree that nationalized many multi-national companies. Although this was forceful acquisition of the assets of others, an after effect of this was that many Nigerians woke up to the idea of becoming business owners. Businesses became more and more indigenous. Solidarity too cannot be something we look up only to the Northern Hemisphere to carry out, in terms of Overseas Direct Assistance(ODA) from foreign government sources, donations and grants from international church organisations and foundations, well-meaning individuals. We must appreciate the efforts of aid groups and individuals who gave generously over the years to people they never even met but solidarity has to be indigenized and organised. We should key into a vision which, much as the Nigerian church began to send missionaries overseas, we would have to start pooling resources to respond in solidarity towards alleviating the plight of less endowed churches in Nigeria and within the sub-continent in a consistent way. This is what the Bishops want Caritas Nigeria to be eventually, a channel of solidarity.

In many parts of the Catholic world, the official Non-Governmental Organisation (NGO) dedicated to social services is called Caritas. For instance there is Catholic Relief Services, which is the American Caritas, Catholic Fund for Overseas Development (CAFOD), which is the Caritas of the English and Welsh Bishops, Caritas Italiana, Caritas Spain, etc. In 2009 Nigerian Bishops instituted a committee to review the CORAT report on the restructuring of Church and Society Department of the Catholic Secretariat of Nigeria (CSN) and recommended the establishment of a relief and development agency as part of Church and Society department. This is what has resulted into Caritas Nigeria or Catholic Caritas Foundation of Nigeria (CCFN) as it is formally called. CCFN is Caritas Nigeria. The Bishops have taken responsibility right at the top by constituting the Board of Trustee. The president of the Conference, his vice, and the secretary of the CBCN are the Trustee. The Board of Directors is chaired by a Bishop, although it also has another Bishop, two priests and four lay persons.

The Bishops Want A Revolution

What the Bishops want with Caritas Nigeria is nothing short of a revolution. It is however a different kind of revolution. According to Pope Benedict the XVl, "Christ does not propose a revolution of a social or political kind, but a revolution of love, brought about by his complete self-giving through his death on the Cross and his resurrection."[3](Africae Munus ,no. 26). It is true that no matter what our condition is, there may be others worse off, and no matter how poor we are, there is still something we can give. The Bishops project CCFN as that platform that will enhance the dignity of the African, a movement towards the self-discovery that each one, no matter how economically impoverished, is a gift and should be a gift unto another. This is why the CBCN set up Caritas Nigeria, so it could be the agency that coordinates the social services of the Church in Nigeria. The Bishops are saying that just as we used to receive funds from overseas through the various agencies set up by the Bishops of those countries, we are now mature enough to have our own agency which will raise funds within the country to support solidarity first within Nigeria and then within the sub-continent. Caritas Nigeria should have a pool of funds that could respond to emergencies and even support development interventions in less endowed dioceses.

A Necessary Shift in Mentality

The above revolution cannot take place without a mental shift. Nigerians are generous. Often however this generosity is directed towards visible projects within the immediate community, such as church buildings, priests' residences and parish halls. It is also a generosity directed towards the extended family, community members, and acquaintances. The truth is that an income earner in Nigeria is responsible not just for his or her nuclear family but a host of others who place expectations on them. This makes it difficult to have spare income that one could dedicate to causes that are beyond the immediate community.

Nevertheless we Nigerians could stretch this generosity a bit more with an appropriate mental shift. There are many who after meeting the needs of the immediate community could still reach out beyond. A Nigerian lady once came from the United States to set up a foundation working to promote awareness on sickle cell. I read her frustrations in a newspaper as she lamented about the poor response from Nigerians. Many Nigerians read newspapers and see gory pictures of children that require help; they may express pity, wag their heads, and open the next page. They may hear about calamities in the North or in the West or South East of the nation but it has not just yet become part of the culture to write a cheque and post it to an address, or give authorization to the bank to remit funds into an advertised account as part of fund-raising to support a cause. The average Nigerian must see the beneficiary physically ! The matter becomes quite compounded with the sophistry Nigerians have variously manifested in exploiting the sense of compassion through many fraudulent claims.

The challenge now is to realize that while we continue to be generous in providing pastoral infrastructure in our environment, we are now also mandated to contribute substantially to works of charity that are far away in other dioceses and even in other lands consistently, not waiting until there is an emergency appeal. We could use the Lenten collection as a starting point, and really be generous in our contributions. According to the Encyclical Letter of Pope Benedict XVl Caritas in Veritate, "Charity in truth places man before the astonishing experience of gift. Gratuitousness is present in our lives in many different forms, which often go unrecognized because of a purely consumerist and utilitarian view of life."[4]

Each person has this gratuitous capacity. It is abundantly present in the average Nigerian. Those set as leaders, such as Bishops, priests, catechists etc would enhance this gift therefore by fanning it into a fire that burns beyond the locality. Rather than limit our people to only what happens within their locality, it is good to turn their attention to the solidarity the Bishops intend to build through the establishment of an agency such as Caritas Nigeria. Priests are key to ensuring this mentality shift.

Underlying Principles

Basic principles underlying the conceptual framework include Common Good, Solidarity and Subsidiarity. The catholicity of our faith ensures that there is opportunity for everyone to responsibly enjoy fullness of life in Christ, even the very poor ones. This is a common good, and sometimes demands sacrifice on everyone's part. We must remember that the poor have no access until we create this access; in solidarity we accept that we are all parts of one body and need to work in communion, while our subsidiarity guarantees us the right to undertake issues at our level without undue interference from a higher level, and yet having enough integrity in what we do such that we are not compelled to be responsible. God loves a cheerful giver. A combination of the three principles above and more will provide enough foundation for the average Nigerian to reach out to someone he may never even meet.

Challenges

The greatest challenge is the tendency to not regard national issues as of high priority. Parishes more often are concerned with what is locally urgent rather than what may be important to the entire Nigerian Church. But this could be overcome by reminding ourselves constantly of our communion and solidarity.

The second challenge is to keep reminding ourselves that an indicator of our faithfulness to the Lord Jesus is how faithful we are with money, which the Lord Jesus described as a 'tainted thing.' We are stewards who render accounts to the Master. As the Lord advised in Luke 16: 9, "use money, tainted as it is, to win you friends..." We can win friends that will enhance our case in eternity. Because of our contribution someone far away would have access to a borehole, go to school, be treated of an ailment, start a small business. And the Lord Jesus will say "So long as you did this to the least of my brethren, you did it unto me...' One could win eternity by supporting Caritas Nigeria to support the underprivileged.

The greatest challenge is that people contribute towards what is known. Caritas Nigeria is still not well known enough. There have been media campaigns through radio jingles and television spots, and millions of SMS have been sent out to mobile phone network subscribers. But this is like acting on the surface without getting to the roots. There needs to be an awareness that begins at the grassroots and towers upwards. One way may be for the Catholic Bishops Conference to adopt a Caritas Week which is celebrated nationally in all the dioceses, simultaneously. During this week, activities around Giving-in-solidarity could be organized. The emphasis during this week would be on giving for solidarity actions that are beyond the local community. A collection could be taken during this week, which is sent to the national Caritas, with the obligation of reporting what was done with the support. In the

United Kingdom, the Bishops of England and Wales hold two collections in support of CAFOD, which is their own Caritas. The American Catholic Bishops also have authorized Catholic Relief Services, which is a part of their own Caritas, to raise funds once a year for the Rice Bowl initiative. In Germany, although MISEREOR is not a member of Caritas, collections are taken every Sunday of Lent in all parishes, and sent directly to MISEREOR for its work around the world, while the German government matches every Euro that is raised. Caritas Germany has its funding mainly through Church tax (government imposes tax on every faith adherent which it hands over to the churches), federal government grants, grants from the European union, membership dues from diocesan Caritas, and donations which are given during an emergency.

While advocacy continues, in making African governments see the need of supporting church agencies like Caritas Nigeria to serve and empower the poor, the Church has to take complete ownership of its own agencies by instituting and supporting structures that sustain its works. So far the Church in Nigeria does the Lenten Collections, which are taken during Stations of the Cross devotion, and on the 5th Sunday of Lent; 20% of these collections are then sent to the national office. Among 56 dioceses, less than half usually send this percentage; the national Caritas therefore has to keep relying on the solidarity of other nations. Meanwhile many diocesan institutions keep sending appeals for assistance to the national Caritas! Many who contribute during the Lenten Collections may not even know how the funds are shared, and the name of Caritas may not even come up, so Caritas still exists in the air somewhat.

It might be a good thing for conferences of Bishops in Africa to examine the number of statutory collections taken nationally per annum and find out whether there is a specific collection for charity. If this does not exist, instituting such a collection might go a long way in entrenching in the consciousness of the faithful an obligation to support a national charity program like Caritas. While the faithful raise funds in millions for physical pastoral projects such as church buildings, priests' residences, etc the leadership of the church should facilitate a mental adjustment to the fact that meting humanitarian and human development needs are also part of the mission of the church.

References

[1] Benedict XVl, (2011). Post Synodal Exhortation Africae Munus of His Holiness Pope Benedict XVl To the Bishops, Clergy, Consecrated Persons and Lay Faithful on the Church in Africa in Service to Reconciliation, Justice and Peace. no. 86

[2] *ibid. 24*

[3] Africae Munus, no. 26)

[4] Benedict XVl, Charity in Truth, no. 34

CHAPTER NINETEEN

THE 2030 SUSTAINABLE DEVELOPMENT GOALS AND HUMAN TRAFFICKING

Introduction

When I think of the important steps that have united humanity, my mind goes back to the formation of the United Nations and especially the Universal Declaration of human rights in 1948, which Pope John Paul ll in addressing the United Nations in 1995, remarked that it remained "one of the highest expressions of the human conscience of our time…'[1]

That declaration was indeed a maturation point in the history of humanity; where as a body of rational beings, leaders of humanity sat together and agreed that there was need for standards with which the dignity of the human person would be protected, as it was now possible to seek redress for infringements, where the state or powerful groups or individuals would not resort to might as right, and even the weakest and ailing members of the human race would be powerful enough through the law, to resist subjugation by politically exposed and economically advantaged persons.

Of course there were no goals and targets and indicators set down to measure compliance. But it was enough at that time, that nations that wanted to remain part of the United Nations had to abide by certain standards of human rights compliance. Many of

175

the nations which became independent adopted these declarations as part of their constitutional provisions. The establishment of the international criminal court of justice also raised the stakes against those who would hide under the canopy of autonomy of states to perpetrate crimes against humanity.

The 2030 sustainable development agenda are another great human stride, another high "expression of the human conscience". By their very vision, we see the conceptualisation of a world moving towards being one human family, where there is concerted action against conditions that impoverish and alienate the human being from the dignity s/he possesses by virtue of being human. If the Universal Declaration of Human Rights have sought to attest that the human being has dignity, these agenda aim at concretizing that dignity, especially for the most marginalised and vulnerable; "they seek to realize the human rights of all and to achieve gender equality and the empowerment of all women and girls... They are integrated and indivisible and balance the three dimensions of sustainable development: the economic, social and environmental."[2]

We read therefore inter alia that its vision is " *a world of universal respect for human rights and human dignity, the rule of law, justice, equality and non-discrimination; of respect for race, ethnicity and cultural diversity; and of equal opportunity permitting the full realization of human potential and contributing to shared prosperity. A world which invests in its children and in which every child grows up free from violence and exploitation. A world in which every woman and girl enjoys full gender equality and all legal, social and economic barriers to their empowerment have been removed. A just, equitable, tolerant, open and socially inclusive world in which the needs of the most vulnerable are met. "[2]* (Transforming Our World, no. 8).

This is a tall and ambitious vision that is meant to be realized through 169 targets which lead up to 17 Goals. The idea is that if nations take the advocacy of Pope Francis seriously, where he advised the United Nations at its 2015 General Assembly to transit from a declarational nominalism to being an effective instrument for real change, then these agenda as negotiated and agreed upon, would take the world to another level if conscientiously implemented.

According to David Nabarro the Special Adviser on the SDGs, "… we find that even some of the wealthiest countries in the world have major inequities when it comes to (these) basic needs. So in summary, this is a universal agenda for all people, for every country and in that respect: Every country is a developing country."[3]

Here in this presentation, our main concern is how anti-human trafficking or the new slavery fares within this agenda and how the provisions in the SDGs could be a framework of action for citizens, institutions and governments at all levels especially in such countries as Nigeria that have become notorious over this scourge. I am assuming that there is awareness on the year 2000 Palermo Protocol which in its article 3 identified elements that constitute human trafficking to include: the exploitation of the prostitution of others, or other forms of sexual abuse, forced labour or enslavement or servitude, and body organ removal. The exploitation of children whether for sex, for labour, including forced begging is seen as trafficking.

Human Trafficking in Nigeria

I suppose we could say that where there is greater economic prosperity a country is more likely to be a place of destination, and where there is prolonged depression in the economy, a country is more likely to be a place of origin in terms of human trafficking. Within itself regions of a country become places of origin and destination, depending on their economic indices and cultural values. In Nigeria everybody knows that trafficking for sexual purposes is more prevalent in Edo State as a place of origin; probably up to 90% of Nigerian women trafficked overseas have a connection to Edo State as a point of origin, even if they are natives of other states. Years ago when the Nigerian economy and therefore the Nigerian currency was valued at more than the United States' dollars, Edo people, especially women were astute in doing business in Europe especially Italy. But the structural adjustment program of the Babangida administration came, occasioned by the downturn in the economy in the 80's. The consequent high exchange rate and the inflation caused by it made many of these businesses to stall. This coincided with demand for unskilled labour in Southern Europe and so there were many immigrations into Italy. At first there was nepotism about it because it was relatives inviting relatives or people inviting those from their communities. This accounts for why there has been a preponderance of Edo people. The discovery that there was high demand for paid sexual services, with more lucrative returns than the menial employment led to the rise in the exploitation of the prostitution of others. While older immigrants facilitated the immigration of neophytes who did not know that they were being trafficked for prostitution, the lid was later blown open and it became common knowledge that Nigerian girls making their way to Italy had every likelihood of being trafficked. But this knowledge has not deterred the crime, which has been sustained through various means of holding people in bondage, including threat to life.

Within Nigeria, Lagos is notorious as a city of destination for in-country trafficking for sexual exploitation. This does not preclude other big cities such as Port Harcourt, Owerri, Kano, as relatives who want the good life for their wards and send them to acquaintances in the cities sometimes do not know what they have bargained for.

Trafficking in Nigeria manifests itself not only in sexual exploitation but organ trafficking, child labour, including domestic exploitation and for begging; the phenomenon of child soldiers has also manifested itself in the last four years with the escalation of Boko Haram terrorism.

In Nigeria organ trafficking is not about transplantation, it is mostly about unorthodox 'medicine' or voodoo. Somehow a set of people believe that they could use human parts for certain rituals that would make them rich or invincible. So children, adult women and men are sometimes kidnapped and killed for body parts which are trafficked for ritual purposes. The most gruesome one was a child who lured another, killing him and removing the intestines, although he was caught in the process.

Another manifestation is new-born child trafficking or what is called baby harvesting. Traffickers could set up fake 'safe houses' where girls with unwanted pregnancies live, give birth and give off their babies to childless couples. What they may not know is that the owners of the centre receives financial rewards for the transactions. This is clearly different than adoption. In some of the rings that have been busted by the police and reported in the media, some young women have taken it as a trade to get pregnant and sell off the babies afterwards. Recently five young pregnant women were arrested for intent on selling their babies on delivery, to the owner of a baby factory[4]. Childless couples are a ready market for trafficked babies, as they go all out to look for babies. Some women go to the extent of pretending to be pregnant, preparatory to 'acquiring' (not adopting) a baby. Some may pay between two to three thousand dollars for a 'baby,' aided by quack clinics. The heavy emphasis on children as an indicator for a successful marriage places heavy burdens on couples, especially the woman, as most Nigerian cultures believe the cause of childlessness resides in the woman, and the woman becomes stigmatized by her in-laws.

A more worrisome dimension is that of 'self-trafficking', where in spite of the enormous sensitization made by NAPTIP, the church and other stakeholders some young women still prefer the associated risks involved, with the hope that after all the exploitation would come the gain of a decent house back home, a car, and support for family members. Those who cross over take pictures and send back home through social media, stirring a hunger in the hearts of prospective candidates. This has an impact too on the smuggling of migrants(SOM), as prospective persons are made to believe that no matter how bad the conditions, they cannot be as terrible as the ones they are currently suffering back in Nigeria, with no employment, no social safety net, no future. So whether as migrants for decent work in Europe or as trafficked sex workers, people submit themselves to the alienation. This is a process of self-dehumanization, a kind of materialism which devalues the self. In this wise the Palermo definition for human trafficking which overrides the consent of such persons is a great foresight, as these women who give their consent to be trafficked would still be seen as victims because of the exploitation of their prostitution by others.

SDGs and Human Trafficking

Among the 17 SDGs, several goals directly bear on the issue of human trafficking. These are: Goals 5 on Gender, 8 on sustainable economic growth and decent work, Goal 10 on reducing inequality, and Goal 16 on inclusive societies, access to justice and building strong institutions. Under these goals, specific targets mention trafficking. These are :

Target 5.2   which aims at eliminating "all forms of violence against all women and girls in the public and private spheres, including trafficking and sexual and other types of exploitation. "

Target 8.7 aims to take   "immediate and effective measures to eradicate forced labour, end modern slavery and human trafficking and secure the prohibition and elimination of the worst forms of child labour, including recruitment and use of child soldiers, and by 2025 end child labour in all its forms;

Target 10.7 Facilitate orderly, safe, regular and responsible migration and mobility of people, including through the implementation of planned and well-managed migration policies

Whereas Target 16.2 aims at ending "abuse, exploitation, trafficking and all forms of violence against and torture of children."

When we run the targets in all the goals, we find that many more address the issue of trafficking in persons, being that they address the fundamental causes which in turn facilitate the overall purpose of the SDGs - which is to give dignity to all humanity in a safe and secure planet, especially those who have been at the receiving end of vulnerability and exploitation. Tackling the fundamental causes through advancing all the goals which are seen as integrated and indivisible would impact positively against the inhuman phenomenon.

Causes of Trafficking in Persons in Nigeria:

According to a 2015 report entitled "Nigeria Sex Trafficking of

Women" produced by the European Asylum Support Office(EASO):

> While economic hardship and limited employment opportunities remain important determinants in today's sex trafficking in Nigeria, sources emphasise the role of multiple co-existing factors, such as: illiteracy, the discrimination and violence faced by women in Nigerian society, the disruption of support systems (loss of family members, for example) , but also the desire to support one's family or 'the desire for greater autonomy and adventure, divorce, love, and familial expectations'. Other factors that have contributed to the growth of the trafficking phenomenon are restrictive migratory policies in Europe, corruption, and to a certain extent a 'strong hold and belief in certain aspects of traditional African religion'"[5].

One would add that the ready market for trafficking, facilitated by the failure to criminalise the patronage by end users is a major cause. Where end users are punished by law, the likelihood exists to find a drop in the percentage of trafficked women.

In Nigeria the economic scenario of the early 80's is playing itself all over again in 2016, with Nigeria dropping from being the largest economy in Africa to being in a recession. Low oil earnings have led to job losses and devaluation of the local currency, leading to high import bills in an economy that imports most of its needs. Poverty and a deep sense of pessimism with regard to the future of work are already adding to increases in the smuggling of migrants, which has the potential of leading to trafficking in persons.

The cultural practice of entrusting children to well to do relatives or acquaintances for care and or for domestic help continues to exacerbate the issue of child abuse and labour. This might likely increase with the economic hardship, as even parents put their children through child labour. On 11th August 2016, ten boys and six girls who hawk food items along the highway in Calabar, were interviewed; 95% of them are in school, 80% of them live with their parents while the rest live with care givers they call Auntie. It was striking to note that as late as 10pm, these children were still in the streets hawking peanuts and garden eggs. Poverty has made parents exploit their children for basic needs. The media have already reported two instances where parents left their kids as collateral, when they couldn't afford the cost of food[6]. To poverty and culture add ignorance, greed, vanity, warped values and you will see a situation where some human beings objectify others and reduce them to transactional status. I would also add that there seems to be a basic orientation in the average Nigerian which colours his/her perception of anything foreign as better, and therefore the scarcity of resources that is made more so by a lack of distributive justice, would continue to push young Nigerian women across the seas for want of a better life, even if they have to become slaves in the process.

Using Some SDG Indicators as Framework of Action

While in Rome two years ago, a Nigerian nun working with trafficked Nigerian women attested in frustration that once they cross into Europe, and get into the business, there is nothing anyone says to them that has effect. She was crying that there were only three solutions: Prevention! Prevention! Prevention!

I believe the SDGs provide a platform to address fundamental issues which give rise to self-dehumanisation or the exploitation of others. The SDG indicators provide milestones for the state and all stakeholders to examine society and rebuild it with a purpose and fervor that would eliminate those structures that leave some at the fringes, structures which John Paul ll referred to as structures of sin, the after effect of which Pope Francis calls a throw away culture. We must ask why there continues to be an influx of trafficked young Nigerian women into Italy for sexual exploitation. IOM has reported crisis level increases in number of trafficked Nigerian women from Libya into Italy, nearly doubling that of last year.[7]

I have therefore selected a few relevant indicators, which should form the basis for action. In deed the solution is good governance. The media have been awash with stories of huge sums of public funds converted to private property through corrupt means by Nigerian public officials. These monies if appropriately used to improve public infrastructure and to set up social safety nets, would reduce the desperation which some people feel about going abroad.

For me therefore indicator 16.4.1* which talks about the *total value of inward and outward illicit financial flows* valued in US dollars is a priority. This indicator monitors target 16.4 which talks about the significant reduction by 2030 in illicit financial flows… and strengthening the recovery of stolen assets, as well as combating organized crime.

 One could only imagine what an inflow of say 200 billion US dollars would do to the Nigerian economy at this time, as it is reported that the United Arab Emirates alone hold about 200 billion US dollars worth of stolen Nigerian assets.[8] Imagine what an investment of this nature into tourism- access- infrastructure could do. Nations in Europe, Asia and North America must clearly show a commitment to the realization of the SDGs by freeing up stolen Nigerian assets hidden within their financial systems. We suggest that just as debt forgiveness came with the conditionality of meting some MDGs, recovered assets should be returned with the conditionality of committing to some SDG targets. In-country recovery efforts should also be supported through forensic investigations, as it does appear that a regime averse to financial corruption is in place in Nigeria and could make good use of the resources. Such recovered assets could be ploughed into the development of infrastructure, as poor infrastructure and poor access to basic services likely contributes to the great sense of alienation which leads to human trafficking. A recent publication of the Sustainable Development Report showed a link between infrastructural development and inequality, as represented below. The development of infrastructure certainly creates access to basic services and therefore reduces inequality. Infrastructural development would contribute to Goal 9 especially target 9.1. with the indicator of *Share of the rural population who live within 2 km of an all-season road(9.1.1).*

Figure I
Evidence map of the infrastructure-inequality-resilience nexus

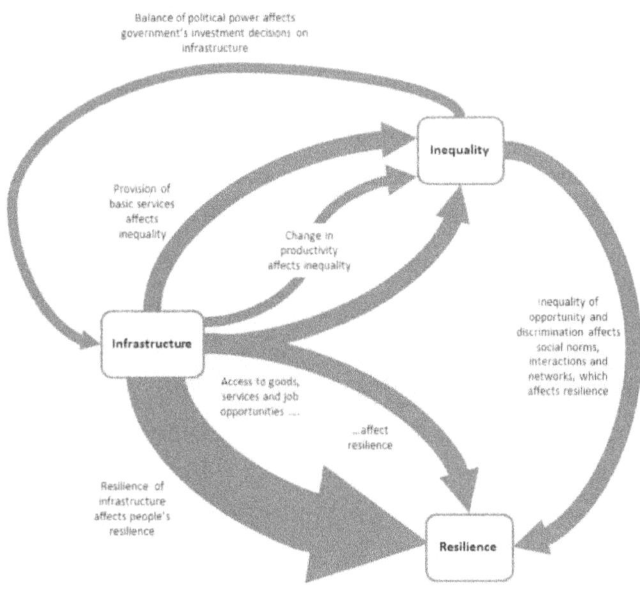

In another wise, Indicator 10.4.1 which monitors the labour share of GDP, comprising wages and social transfers, under target 10.4 which talks about adopting "policies, especially fiscal, wage and social protection policies, and progressively achieve greater equality;" would be for me another area of priority. This also ties with indicator 8.b.1   which monitors *Total government spending in social protection and employment programmes as a percentage of the national budgets and GDP.*

The Nigerian government proposed a 500 billion naira amount in the 2016 budget for some kind of social safety net, for unemployed graduates, micro finance access for women etc. As this issue of trafficking has become a global embarrassment for Nigeria, it is important to target the key populations in this respect and take measures that would stem the tide of trafficking. Care givers of children especially women should be targeted for full time housewife status benefits; an assessment should also be conducted of girls in these catchment areas who should be monitored to complete secondary education and university education, or put into financial literacy and entrepreneurship programs that would guarantee starter packs for small businesses.   In deed free education for girls up to university level should be adopted as a national mitigating measure. A properly educated woman would not submit herself to be trafficked. An investment in education for girls would not only promote Goal 4(education for all) but Goal 5 (gender equality) and Goal10 (reduce inequality) as well. If the allocative efficiency of states and federal government budgets could be improved upon, by increasing transparency and reducing the corruption integrated into government budgets, there would be enough resources to do this in spite of the down turn in the economy.

Countries that intend to return Nigeria's stolen assets could also put it as a precondition, the free education of girls from upper secondary to university level, and the non-formal education and training of young women in catchment areas of such trafficking. Enforceable, free and compulsory education of the girl-child to university level and or creating compulsory access to non-formal business and life skills education and easy access to credit may also help monitor indicator 5.3.1 to determine *Percentage of women aged 20-24 who were married or in a union before age 15 and before age 18.*

The final suggestion for me, would be monitoring indicator 10.7.3 (under Target 10.7) that has to do with *Number of detected and non-detected victims of human trafficking per 100,000 population, by sex, age group and form of exploitation.*

Nigerian authorities would have to do more in terms of joint initiatives with other countries to monitor migration routes. The gory stories of what people go through: dying of thirst in the desert and drinking one's urine, eating human carcasses, corpses littering the desert *sandscape* without funerals, capsized boats and drowned lives.... If as reported, that 80% of Nigerian girls that go to Italy are for sex trafficking purposes, there should be stronger collaboration between Nigerian authorities and Italian authorities, for the identification of Nigerian girls on arrival and their immediate debriefing and repatriation; for once they start the illicit trade, it is difficult to break off. Government should therefore support NGOs on returnee programs.

The porous nature of Nigerian borders not only facilitates trafficking but gives room for the insecurity of the nation. The menace of Fulani herdsmen who have enormous capacity to sack whole communities, is exacerbated by the fact that many of them come in from neighbouring countries through these porous borders.

The Greatest Challenge:

The greatest challenge remains the weakness of state institutions, made more so by the cultures and traditions of our various ethnic nationalities. Where under age marriages are custom and the girl-child could be abducted, proselytized and married and the state is helpless in the face of it, it weakens the confidence of citizens to rely on state institutions to fight against trafficking and all kinds of violence against women.

A way to resolve this is for the church to intensify advocacy with socially exposed traditional rulers and engage them to work towards changing some norms and values of the traditional system. Where these are based on religion, it becomes somewhat more difficult but still not impossible to engage.

The onus also lies on the church, to intensify prevention messages, not only from the altar but as part of evangelizing outreaches in communities. Whenever possible, the church through Caritas, should raise funds from its membership and support families with training on income generating activities, with access to micro finance. Targeting young girls and organizing programs that expose to them the dangers of human trafficking should be joint efforts by parishes and if possible, collaborative initiatives with local government authorities. Efforts should be made to capture stories of victims and present these to would be victims.

There should be a call to action in Edo State, which government often lives in denial. Edo government should work with traditional institutions and the church to change the psyche of the people.

Conclusion:

The quest for upholding the dignity of the human person promises to remain an engaging war, not a battle that is won in one front. Even though dignity should be a given, being itself the gift of God, yet historically it has had to be fought for and defended, as powers that be often assume they should exploit and alienate the dignity of others. This becomes worse when state institutions are weak and lose the monopoly of violence and when citizens become lethargic and give away their sovereignty. The struggle for good governance is therefore the struggle for dignity. Jesus said I came that they may have life and have it to the full. No human being has the right to stand between the fullness of life of another, which is his dignity.

REFERENCES

United Nations Charter [Online] Available from http://www.un.org/en/documents/charter/chapter1.shtml [Accessed 12/9/2015], Art 1.

Transforming Our World: The 2030 Agenda For Sustainable Development Outcome Document For The Un Summit To Adopt The Post-2015 Development Agenda. Finalised Text for Adoption July 31 [Online] Available from https://sustainabledevelopment.un.org/.../... [Accessed on 12/08/2016], Preamble 1.1.

Navarro, D. (2016) A Conversation with Special Adviser on the 2030 Agenda David Nabarro about Sustainable Development and Conflict Prevention. 6th July 2016. New York United Nations. [ONLINE] Available from globaldaily.com/every-country-is-a-developing-country-an-interview-david-nabarro-on-sustainable—development-and-conflict-prevention [Accessed on 3-08-2016]

Onoyume, J. (2016) Police Arrest 5 Pregnant Women with Plans to Sell Babies on Delivery. *Guardian Newspaper.* 24/5/2016

European Union. European Asylum Support Office (2015). *Nigeria Sex Trafficking of Women.*

Punch Newspapers. (2016) Man Abandons Son for Bag of Rice in Kano. 27/7/2016

The Guardian Newspapers. Trafficking of Nigerian Women into Prostitution in Europe 'at Crisis Level'. 8/8/2016.

Premium Times. Panic Grips Nigerian Corrupt Officials as Buhari Signs Agreement on Stolen Funds from the United Arab Emirates. [Online] Available from www.premiumtimesng.com/.../197063-panic-grips-corrupt-**nigerian**-officials-as-buhari.signs.agreement.on.stolen.funds.from.united.arab.emirate.html [Accessed on 8/8/2016

BIBLIOGRAPHY

AFRICA'S COMMITMENT (Africae Munus).Post-Synodal Apostolic Exhortation of His Holiness Pope Benedict XVI to the Bishops, Clergy, Consecrated Persons and the Lay Faithful on the Church in Africa in Service to Reconciliation, Justice and Peace.(Nairobi:Paulines Publications Africa,2011).

ARCHBISHOP IGNATIUS KAIGAMA, Personal testimony, President of Nigerian Bishops Conference, December 2014

BAEDE, A.P.M. et al. Climate System: An Overview. [Online] Accessed from www.grida.no/climate/ipcc.../tar-01.pdf   [Accessed on July 6th 2015]

BENTON, A . (2015) Nepal Earthquake Could Have Been a Manmade Disaster As Climate Change Brings Seismic Shift. *Newsweek Magazine.* 08.05.2015 no 19

CAMPBELL, J. (2014) *Boko Haram: origins, challenges and responses.* Norwegian Peacebuilding Resource Centre [Online] October 2014 . Available from www.peacebuilding.no/.../original/.../... [Access 13th July 2015]

COUNTRY METERS. *Nigeria Population Clock.* [Online] Available from www.countrymeters.info/en/Nigeria [Accessed 13th July 2015]

EDWARD CHAMBERS WITH MICHAEL COWEN, *Roots for Radicals: Organisng for Power,Action and Justice*, (New York: The Continuum International Publishing Group, 2003),p.27

ELISABETH ROSENTHAL, New York Times 14th April 2012

EUROPEAN UNION. EUROPEAN ASYLUM SUPPORT OFFICE (2015). *Nigeria Sex Trafficking of Women.*

EVARISTUS BASSEY, Caritas Stylus, a Caritas Nigeria Newsletter Dec 2014

FAO Module 1 Understanding Climate Variability and Climate Change. [Online] Accessed from ftp://ftp.fao.org/docrep/.../a1247e02.pdf [Accessed on July 6th 2015]

FEDERAL MINISTRY OF ENVIRONMENT. [Online] . Accessed from http://www.climatechange.gov.ng/index.php/fme/special-fme-units. [Accessed on 7th July 2015].

FUKAYAMA, F. (2014) *Political Order and Political Decay.* London: Profile Books.

http://.m.sparknotes.com/.../Aristotle/section10...
http://nigeria.opendataforafrica.org/ljnupce/nigeria-food-access

http://www.ifpri.org/publication/ensuring-food-and-nutrition-security-rural-nigeria

http://www.marineandpetroleum.com/node/80

IBEABUCHI, C. (2012) Religious Bodies, NGOs must Pay Tax for Trading Subsidiaries, FRC insists. Vanguard, Lagos

INGAWA, S. A, G.TARAWALI, R.VON KAUFMANN, Grazing Reserves in Sub-humid Nigeria, ILCA , Addis Ababa, 1989 Network paper no.22

INTERGOVERNMENTAL PANEL ON CLIMATE CHANGE. *Climate Change 2007: Synthesis Report.* Valencia: IPCC Plenary XXVll. p.(30) [Online]. Accessed from www.ipcc.ch/.../assessment-report/... [Accessed on July 6th 2015].

INTERNATIONAL STANDARD VERSION BIBLE

IPCC, 2014: Summary for Policymakers. In :*Climate Change 2014: Impacts, Adaptation and Vulnerability .Part A: Global and Sectoral Aspects. Contribution of Working Group ll to the Fifth Assessment*

Report of the Intergovernmental Panel on Climate Change. Field, C.B.et al (eds). Cambridge and New York: Cambridge University Press.

JOSIE COX, Wall Street Journal Dec 19, 2014

KOLEHAMAINEN-AIKEN** RL: **Decentralization and human resources: implications and impact.**Human Resources for Health Development Journal 1997, **2(1):1-14.

LAWAL, B. T. (2013) The Charitable and Private Non-Profit Organisations in Nigeria and their Tax Obligations, Federal Inland Revenue Service Workshop, Abuja

MONITORING GROWTH AND RESILIENCE IN CHILDREN developed in conjunction with Nutrition for Health and Development(NHD) and Sustainable Development and Healthy Environments(SDE), *p.3*

National Health Bill Art. 1(e), 3(3)

National Health Bill Art. 11 (3a)

National Health Bill Art. 11 (3e)

National Health Bill Art. 18(2)

NAVARRO, D. (2016) A Conversation with Special Adviser on the 2030 Agenda David Nabarro about Sustainable Development and Conflict Prevention. 6th July 2016. New York United Nations. [ONLINE] Available from globaldaily.com/every-country-is-a-developing-country-an-interview-david-nabarro-on-sustainable—development-and-conflict-prevention [Accessed on 3-08-2016]

NIGERIA DEMOGRAPHICS PROFILE, http://www.indexmundi.com/nigeria/demographics_profile.html

NIGERIA. FEDERAL MINISTRY OF ENVIRONMENT. *National Environmental(Domestic and Industrial Plastic, Rubber and Foam Sector* S.I. No.17 of 2011. Art.2

NIGERIA. FEERAL MINISTRY OF ENVIRONMENT. *National Environmental (Control of Vehicular Emissions from Petrol and Diesel Engines) Regulations, 2011.*Art.1

NIGERIA.FEDERAL MINISTRY OF ENVIRONMENT. *National Environmental(Control of Bush, Forest Fire and Open Burning) Regulations, 2011.* Part 1, no.1 S.I. No.15 of 2011.

NOTE 1. The idea of a Fund while being original, the framework is based on the research carried out by the International Center for Non Profit law in 2010

NOTE 2. A study of the Fund has been carried out in thirteen countries. The countries are Albania, Azerbaijan, Croatia, Hungary, Kazakhstan, Jordan, Poland, South Africa, Turkey, Estonia, Sweden, the United Arab Emirates and the United Kingdom.

OLUSEGUN, K.T. (2013) Value Added Tax (VAT) Administration in Nigeria: The Role of Charitable and Private Non-Profit Organisations, Federal Inland Revenue Service Workshop, Abuja

ON THE DEVELOPMENT OF PEOPLES (Populorum Progressio). Encyclical Letter of His Holiness Pope Paul VI. (Nairobi: Paulines Publications Africa,1990)

ONI, I.O. (2008) Nigerian Companies Income Tax (Law and Practice)

ONOYUME, J. (2016) Police Arrest 5 Pregnant Women with Plans to Sell Babies on Delivery. *GUARDIAN NEWSPAPER.* 24/5/2016

OXFORD ADVANCED LEARNER'S DICTIONARY, S.V. Superstition, Oxford University Press, Oxford 7th Edition,2005

PITTOCK, B. (2009) *Climate Change:The Science, Impacts and Solutions.* ,Melbourne: CSIRO Publishers.

POPE BENEDICT XVI, Charity in Truth, no. 34

POPE BENEDICT XVI, Homily for the Solemn Inauguration of the Petrine Ministry(24 april 2005):AAS 97 (2005) 710

POPE BENEDICT XVI, Post Synodal Exhortation Africae Munus of His Holiness To the Bishops, Clergy, Consecrated Persons and Lay Faithful on the Church in Africa in Service to Reconciliation, Justice and Peace (2011)

POPE FRANCIS.(2015) *Laudato Si*. Vatican: Vatican Publications.

POPE JOHN PAUL II, (1987). On Social Concern. Nairobi: Paulines Publication Africa, no.42.

POPE JOHN PAUL II, *Solicitudo Rei Socialis* (Nairobi: Paulines Publications Africa, 2001), no.32

POPE PAUL VI (1990).On New Social Problems. Nairobi: Paulines Publications Africa, no.15

POPE PAUL VI, (1990). On the Development of Peoples. Nairobi: Paulines Publications Africa, no.47

PREMIUM TIMES. Panic Grips Nigerian Corrupt Officials as Buhari Signs Agreement on Stolen Funds from the United Arab Emirates. [Online] Available from www.premiumtimesng.com/.../197063-panic-grips-corrupt-**nigerian**-officials-as-buhari.signs.agreement.on.stolen.funds.from.united.arab.emirate.html [Accessed on 8/8/2016

PUNCH NEWSPAPERS. (2016) Man Abandons Son for Bag of Rice in Kano. 27/7/2016

***RANDOM HOUSE** Kernerman Webster's College Dictionary*. (2010) . London: Random House, Inc.

SALTMAN RB, *Von Otter C: Implementing Planned Markets in Health Care: Balancing Social and Economic Responsibility. Buckingham: Open University Press; 1995.*

SAYNE, A. *Rethinking Nigeria's Indigene-Settler Conflicts.* [Online]. Available from www.usip.org/sites/default/.../SR311.pdf

SECTION 10 of Decree no.38 of 1992 bans broadcast houses for political parties and religious groups.

SERAH, W. (2013) Understanding Withholding Tax (WHT) and the Role of Charitable and Private Non-Profit Organisations in Nigeria, Federal Inland Revenue Service Workshop, Abuja

SHELDON WOLIN, *The Presence of the Past* (Baltimore:johns Hopkins University Press, 1989).

SPECIAL EVENT 25 September: Outcome Document', United Nations General Assembly 2013

STERN, J. BERGER, J.M.(2015) *ISIS The State of Terror.* London:William Collins.

THE CODE OF CANON LAW.(Theological Publications in India, Bangalore, 2005 ed), Canon 1061.

THE GUARDIAN NEWSPAPERS. Trafficking of Nigerian Women into Prostitution in Europe 'at Crisis Level'. 8/8/2016.

THE SUN NEWSPAPER 8 December 2014, Lagos Nigeria

THOMAS BOSSERT *et al : Assessing Financing, Education, Management and Policy Context for Strategic Planning of Human Resources for Health. World Health Organization 2007.*

TRANSFORMING OUR WORLD: THE 2030 AGENDA FOR SUSTAINABLE DEVELOPMENT OUTCOME DOCUMENT FOR THE UN SUMMIT TO ADOPT THE POST-2015 DEVELOPMENT AGENDA. Finalised Text for Adoption July 31 [Online] Available from https://sustainabledevelopment.un.org/.../... [Accessed on 12/08/2016], Preamble 1.1.

TRANSPARENCY INTERNATIONAL. *2014 Corruption Perception Index Measures the Perceived Levels of Public Sector Corruption in 175 Countries and Territories*. #CPI2014.[Online].   Available from http://www.transparency.org/cpi2014. [Accessed on 13th July 2015].

UNFCC Article 1.[Online] Accessed from www.unfcc.int. [Accessed on 6th July 2015].

UNGA Outcome Doc 2013

UNITED   NATIONS   CHARTER [Online] Available from http://www.un.org/en/documents/charter/chapter1.shtml   [Accessed 12/9/2015], Art 1.

VATICAN   COUNCIL   II The Concilliar and Post Concilliar Documents. Austin Flannery,O.P., ed.(Northport: Costello Publishing Company, 1975).

WALL STREET JOURNAL, 7 June 2014
WIKIPEDIA. *National   Identity*. [Online]. Available from https://en.m.wikipedia.org/wiki/National_identity). [Accessed 11th July 2015]

Wikipedia.org/wiki/Samaritans

Wordpress.com/how-hunger-hurts/

www.country-data.com/cgi.../r-10408.ht...
www.unicef.org/.../Nigeria_statistics.html